# leaves
# life from an unexpected
# life

a refugee's journey

"when all I wanted was to sing,
I was accorded with the honor
of living."

—rainer maria rilke

*Three*

# márta anna ilona

*Eighty-nine*

# köváry kilczer blades

for michele,

marika,

and

michael

# circumstances beyond control

## márta blades

Circumstances hemmed me
in a small corner,
hard as I tried
I could not reach the sun,
and I wanted to give you
the sun…

Circumstances chained me
to a mundane world,
hard as I tried
I could not grasp the moon,
and I wanted to give you
the moon…

Circumstances kept my soul
an ambulatory half corpse,
hard as I tried
I could not capture the stars,
and I wanted to give you
the stars…

Circumstances darkened
the whole world
and life stormed,
and it raged,
and it rained,
oh, how it rained…

Circumstances be damned!
with my remaining strength
I gathered
the storm's colors,
and I made you a
rainbow…

And you reached out,
and held on
to the rainbow,
with all its colors,
and climbed until you
touched the untouchable sky…

You found the sun,
and held the moon,
scattered the stars,
across the sky,
and gave me the world…
with love.

Copyright © 2019 by Márta Blades. All rights reserved. Printed in the United States of America. No part of this book may be used or reproduced in any manner whatsoever without written permission except in the case of brief quotations included in critical articles and reviews. For information, address permissions@citrinepublishing.com.

**Limit of Liability/Disclaimer of Warranty:** While the publisher and author have used their best efforts in preparing this book, they make no representations or warranties with respect to the accuracy or completeness of the contents of this book and specifically disclaim any implied warranties of merchantability or fitness for a particular purpose. The views expressed in this work are solely those of the author and do not necessarily reflect the views of the publisher.

*Cover art and layout by Márta Blades*
*Map of Hungary drawn by T.G. Monahan*

**Library of Congress Cataloging-in-Publication Data**

Blades, Márta
Leaves from an Unexpected Life: A Refugee's Journey

p. cm.

Hardcover ISBN: 978-1-947708-37-2
Ebook ISBN: 978-1-947708-38-9
Library of Congress Control Number: 2019914419
First Edition, October 2019

CITRINE PUBLISHING
Murphy, North Carolina, USA
(828) 585-7030
www.CitrinePublishing.com

# dedicated with love to:

the memory of my parents:
Martha Ujtordai Köváry Kilczer and Mihály Kilczer,
who gave me the strengh for life;
my two daughters, my son, and their spouses:
Michele and Jerome Jr.,
Marika and Brian,
Michael and Kathy,
who make my life worthwhile.

# contents

| | |
|---|---|
| xii | **Prologue** |
| xiv | **Hungary and Family History** |
| xvi | **Map** |
| | **Chapters** |
| 1 | Red-Haired Glory |
| 3 | Five Spikes on Her Crown |
| 9 | Some Places Before Szentes |
| 13 | Proudly From the Bánát |
| 18 | No Name Day for Pálma |
| 22 | "But the Region is Beautiful" |
| 27 | French Grace in War |
| 32 | Juhász Gyula's Poem |
| 33 | Hopeless No More |
| 37 | Love, Love, Love Lindau |
| 41 | I Left My Heart in the *Schwabische Alb* |
| 43 | And Then There Were Two |
| 48 | Camping in Grohn |
| 51 | After the War |
| 55 | On the Ocean, in the C.C. Ballou |
| 58 | Good Morning, Sweet Liberty |
| 61 | Marian College |
| 65 | Another Super Angel |
| 67 | And There Was a Rainbow |

# contents

| | |
|---|---|
| 71 | Waiting for the New Year 1972 |
| 76 | Joy at the Emporium |
| 80 | She Was NOT a Bunny Rabbit |
| 84 | Return to Hungary |
| 86 |     Budapest |
| 89 |     Kecskemét |
| 90 |     Szentes |
| 93 |     Herend |
| 96 |     Transylvania |
| 104 | Thirty-Five Glorious Gallery Years |
| 109 | Finally Settling Down in the South |
| 111 | Traded a Kidney For a Dog |
| 115 | 3rd Christmas on the 1st Floor |
| 118 | My Bestest Friend Becomes a Doctor |
| 123 | Real, Real Friends |
| 126 | Return with All Three |
| 133 | Remembering |
| 141 | Acknowledgments |
| 143 | Possibility of a Future |

# prologue

**WHEN I WAS TEN YEARS OLD,** I attended the *Erzsébet Nöiskola* (Elisabeth Women's School), a boarding school in Budapest. My father had studied all the various possibilities in *gymnasiums* (high schools) and found "the *Erzsébet*" best... *serious intelligencia.*

My mother's Aunt Minty in Budapest did not approve. She was mentioning *Le Rosey* in Switzerland (the most "in" school in the world) or a *Lycee de Sacre Coeur (not* the one in Budapest, but one of the eleven in France).

My mother also informed me that Aunt Minty had already started to work on my "Coming Out," just eight years away.

Imagine that. I would be a *debutante...*

It seemed that either way, my father's or Aunt Minty's, the future looked pretty golden.

My life did not work out quite like either way.

When I was fourteen years old, we lost everything, due to a war. *Everything.* We became refugees, with nothing but my mother's jewelry, hidden in her hair.

Then we became American citizens. This blessed country opened its door so generously to so many of us "huddled masses." And I hope that it will do so someday again, soon.

The years seem to have rushed by so fast. I lived through joy, and sadness.

Life turned out longer than I expected while watching three beautiful babies grow into decent, wonderful, amazing adults who gifted me the joy, of

Nonni-ness when I became the grandmother of four wonder-boys. I've lost loved ones and gained the happiest last ten years of my life.

Being able to paint, as much as I wanted, has been *bliss!* Seven exhibits, during ten years. Two were in Indianapolis, five in Winston Salem. The last two were at Sawtooth School for Visual Art and Salem College, the oldest women's college in America.

I feel so honored.

Some stories in this book were more than bittersweet than others to write.

And if "thank you" appears too often, I don't think it appears enough.

I met so many, many people—human angels—along my long way to NOW.

And I am so very, very grateful…

Because, I did not become a *debutante* per Aunt Minty's wish, or a graduate of the University of Oxford or the Universite Paris Sorbonne, which were my father's dreams.

But I have had *an interesting, full life* that I would not change for anything!

I thank you, who walked with me.

Márta Blades
*October, 2019*

# hungary & family history

| | |
|---|---|
| 895 | Conquest of Hungary *(honfoglalas)* at Etelköz. 7 Chieftains, Arpad, the *Kende* (king) |
| 1000 | Coronation of István (Saint Steven), crown a gift from Pope Sylvester II |
| 1458 | Matthias (Mátyás), son of János Hunyady, rebuilds the kingdom, introduces Renaissance culture |
| 1526 | Mohács, Turks defeat Hungarians at battle, control most of the country |
| 1541 | The Sultan occupies Buda |
| 1699 | Peace treaty with Ottoman Empire, end of 158 years of occupation |
| 1740 – 80 | Enlightened reign of Maria Theresa |
| 1887 | Márta's father is born in Temesgyarmata (now Giarmata) |
| 1848 | March 15, Revolution, war of independence |
| 1900 | Márta's mother is born in Kolozsvar (now Cluj) |
| 1917 | Márta's parents are married and live in Vajdahunyad (now Hunadora) |
| 1918 | Defeat, disintegration of Austro-Hungarian Monarch |
| 1920 | Treaty of Trianon divides up central Europe. Hungary loses great part (including Transylvania and the Banat |

| | |
|---:|:---|
| **1920** | Admiral Miklos Horthy elected Hungary's Regent |
| **1920** | Márta's parents leave Transylvania, which had become part of Romania, and flee to Budapest |
| **1930** | Márta is born in Kecskemét |
| **1939** | World War II begins (Hungary with the Axis) |
| **1940** | Márta's family moves from Budapest to Szentes |
| **1944** | Márta and her mother leave Szentes, just before the Soviets arrive |
| **1944–45** | Germany invades Hungary |
| **1945** | End of war, Soviet army enters Hungary |
| **1949** | Márta sails on the C.C. Ballou for America |
| **1950** | Total dictatorship of communist party |
| **1956** | Students protest against communism, against Soviet Army; 200,000 Hungarian exodus |
| **1989** | Proclamation of Hungarian Republic |
| **1990–91** | After forty-five years of domination, the Soviets begin leaving Hungary, with the last troops being withdrawn in June 1991 |
| **1998-2002** | Victor Orbán becomes Prime Minister of Hungary |
| **2010-present** | Victor Orbán re-elected Prime Minister of Hungary |

# hungary (1920) post-treaty of trianon

*With my mother*

## red-haired glory

**NATURALLY BORN** red-headed Hungarians in the 1930s were the rarest of the ruby-crowned ones.

Most of the ladies who carried exotic, somewhat "red" hair on their heads were not born with it... their red came from bottles at beauty shops. They were different "ladies," called "ladies of the evening," or they were "ladies of the theatre." Either way, society placed them in a pretty similar category in those days.

I was a happy three-year-old, naturally born with fiery red hair. Every day, my lovely Austrian governess, *Fraulein* Lotte, put a lovely bonnet on my head and we marched joyously to the beautiful city park for our daily walks in Budapest.

One sunny day, however, I happened to be bonnet-less, enjoying the park's many surprises—colorful flowers, other children with their nannies, butterflies, flora and fauna, the golden sun. What transpired that day was quite surprising. We came face to face with an elegant elderly lady who was wearing a pretty hat and important jewelry. She was obviously a *real* society lady. She looked at me, and then at *Fraulein* Lotte, as she raised her voice to an unladylike high tone.

"What on earth are you doing, dying this child's hair *RED?!*" she cried. "What terrible taste! Just terrible!"

Considering that until then I did not know that I had *terrible* hair, I could not say a word and just reached for Fraulein Lotte's handkerchief, one that was hardly enough for my tears.

Six white horses could not drag me to walk in our beloved park ever again.

leaves from an unexpected life

My parents and I soon moved from Budapest to Southern Hungary, to the sweet small town of Szentes. There I lost my dear governess, *Fraulein* Lotte, but I gained a new adventure, called "school."

I loved school, I loved our house, I loved my new friends.

I loved that nobody ever called my hair "terrible."

That is, until several years later, when I was attending Erzsébet Nöiskola in Budapest. As it happened, one of the boys in our group, named Laci, began to call me "the red frog from Budapest."

But by then, I did not care. I was used to my red hair and sort of liked it. And my quite sophisticated best friend, Ebé, explained to me that "Laci is in love with you…"

We were ten years old.

## five spikes on her crown

ujtordai Keöváry

**MY MOTHER** seldom mentioned her background, whereas my father did. He often teased her, calling her "the princess," which she was not. She only had five spikes on her crowns, carved on her silver, embroidered on her napkins and towels.

"Five spikes are for *kurta nemes,*" she said (literally, *short noble*). "The lowest of the low, of nobility," she explained.

Her grandmother, Kamilla Kendeffy of Malomviz, however, had seven spikes on her crown. My great-grandmother stood higher on the noble ladder—she even lived in a castle!

We did not, because of mother's only five spikes on her crown.

Born Martha Köváry of Ujtorda, she had married a commoner. Not just that, but a commoner from the Bánát, *not* Transylvania. The Bánát was for peasants. The fact that my father was a Ph.D. did not matter at all, not to the Transylvanian nobility. Martha Köváry was wedded to a man who did not have a crown. He had *NO* spikes!

My mother was not terribly interested in the fact that she was a cousin of the Windsors. Well, she was seven times removed from Her Majesty Queen Elisabeth II. Nor was she interested in the fact that she was an ancestor of Prince Vlad Tepes III, the prince, the prince no one liked at all and she despised, the prince who was the model for Dracula.

She did care for the Kövárys. Without all those spikes, they were a very interesting family. Her father, Dr. Ernö, was a renaissance man—doctor, painter sculptor, and breeder of Hungarian Vizsla dogs. He married the beautiful Ilona Köszegvary (Kamilla Kendeffy's daughter) in 1898. My mother was born in 1900, her sister Katalin (Kitty) in 1902.

Madame Köváry (my grandmother) had different interests, none of them related to her husband's. She was a beauty and hoped for a more glamorous, society life that was offered in Kolozsvár (Cluj). The lights of the capitol of Hungary, Budapest, beckoned and she was off.

Divorced.

That was somewhat scandalous in the early 1900s. *And* not only did she choose Budapest, she chose only one of her daughters to go with her. She chose the blue-eyed blonde, Kitty.

"I will be back and will take you, too," she promised my mother.

She never did.

*Dr. Ernö ujtordai Köváry, my grandfather*

My mother was raised by her father and his rather stern unmarried sister, Gizella Köváry. Aunt Gizi told my mother that Kitty was taken by their mother "because she was pretty."

These words my mother, somewhere in the back of her mind, never forgot. Even if she ended up the lucky one. Growing up around the Köváry men—her fencing-champion/lawyer grandfather, Mihály; her uncles Endre, a famous portrait painter, and László, a well-known historian and author—made for a rather interesting and wonderful youth. There is still a street named for Laszlo and a brass plaque on the Köváry house in Kolozsvár (now Cluj).

Meanwhile Aunt Kitty enjoyed the glamor of Budapest. And she ended up outdoing her mother, she had four divorces.

My mother was proud of her common born scientist husband. For her, he and I, her only child were above everything. She made sure my color-blind father always wore matching socks, that my red hair was cut and combed, and that our house and garden were always beautiful. She attended to life's details, she sang, she played her *hegedu* (violin), she laughed, she was happy.

But she did miss the mountains, and Transylvania.

She was beautiful, too. Ramrod bearing and elegant, she had lovely taste. She adored beautiful things, French gowns, and Italian shoes. She enjoyed her precious antique silver, the paintings on the walls, Persian rugs, Herend porcelain, Biedermeier furniture bedecked with intarsia, all inheritances from the Köváry family, and all remnants they were able to save, when they had to leave Transylvania.

After World War I, the Austro-Hungarian Empire was broken up and Transylvania, which had been part of Hungary, became part of Romania. Hungary had new borders and was declared a separate republic. My father was director of the mines in Vajdahunyad, which were owned by the Hungarian government. He packed up everything and everybody who wanted to leave from the mines, and they traveled in a long, long train to Budapest. The trains contained all the things that my father believed belonged to the Hungarian government. So off he went.

For this he was blacklisted, never to be able to return to Transylvania. My parents never saw their beloved country, or families, again. I only knew my relatives through stories.

Our house in Szentes was a joyful place. As was our garden. And mother cared for all these things, almost as much as she cared for my father and me.

And many years, and an ocean later, for my children, her grandchildren.

*My first ballet performance*

## some places before szentes

**ON A STORMY** October day in 1944, my mother locked the door of our house on Toth Jozsef Street in Szentes. I had just turned fourteen.

Little did we know, that for my parents, it was the last time they would see Szentes.

I had to wait forty-eight years, until the Soviets left Hungary in 1991, to see the house in Szentes that I loved so much.

My parents, after they left Transylvania in 1920, when it became Romania, became somewhat nomadic. From Budapest to Kecskemét to Hodmezövásárhely, they moved and finally to Szentes.

Each city had its charm. Mother loved the culture in Budapest. Father opened an engineering office and I was born in Kecskemét.

I have lovely memories of Hodmezövásárhely (do not try to pronounce it!) where father became a public-provision chief inspector. What that had to do with being a mining engineer, only the heavens knew. My godfather however, was Secretary of State, so Father started inspecting provisions.

We lived in a beautiful house in Hodmezövásárhely. And every day we saw a proud, picturesque "four in hand" carriage (pulled by four horses) virtually fly under our windows.

Fairly soon, we met the people enjoying the rides in these carriages. And pretty soon they became my parents' best friends. Uncle Ali was the director of the méntelep, the Royal Hungarian horse farms. His glorious, brilliant wife, Aunt Pálma, became my mother's best friend. Their daughter, Alice, and son, Peter, became my friends. Their family became very special to mine, for the coming many, many years.

When my father was transferred to Szentes, the capital of Csongrád County, we had a hard time finding a house. The one we finally found was not nearly as beautiful as our past homes were. Mother, however, was happier than happy. The garden was huge, and rather neglected. It was not neglected for long. She found every garden tool available, and quite a few gardeners, and there was a gazebo, along with lovely paths, and a rose garden, and bushes, and flowers. Many, many flowers.

We were very happy in Szentes. Once my parents followed the Hungarian "must" in a new city, called "*feszt* visit," a first visit to the town's important inhabitants (never longer than five minutes) our lives became very busy.

Mother joined a bridge group and a book club. I met my best friend, Ebé (to this day my best friend), the lieutenant governor's beautiful daughter, who saw to it, that I learned the dos and don'ts of Szentes. Father, always elegant in suits, ties, hats, and well-shined shoes, walked to his office, joined the *Uri Kaszino* (Gentleman's Casino), where he smoked cigars, played bridge, and met interesting neighbors.

I loved Szentes. I loved our school, and I especially loved the birthday parties, called jours. Summers were lived by "the strand," our swimming pool in the park. I loved the plays we put on. Mother and her friends made wonderful costumes for us. I loved Thursdays, when our staff cleaned silver. It was also Mother's bridge day. I was not allowed in the kitchen, but on Thursdays, the minute the front door closed, I was in the kitchen, "helping" the help polishing silver. (Many, many years later, when I had two sweet daughters who were allowed in the kitchen, and I was the only person polishing the silver, I promised them that if they were very good, they could also polish silver. That, however, did not last long.)

I never found out if my mother knew about my Thursday secret. Our helpers loved her. She lived her quote, "You can always tell a lady by the way she treats the servants."

She was a perfect lady.

*A page from one of my father's inventions*

## proudly from the bánát

**MY FATHER WAS** the most, kind, gentle man. He was also, or bordered on being, a genius.

While working for the Hungarian government as a mining engineer, he had registered several inventions, which they used. When Transylvania became Romania, and he retired, the government declared these inventions as their property. He did not care. He would work on more inventions, he promised my mother. Greed was not even known to him.

He came from a different world from that of my mother. He was born in the Bánát, a part of Hungary that also became Romania after World War I.

The Bánát was more or less created from the marshes in the eighteenth century. Count Claudius Mercy cleaned up the region, which then turned into rich, black fertile soil. The Count and Empress Maria Teresa settled this land with skilled agricultural people from Alsac and Bavaria between 1722 and 1787, to teach the Hungarians agriculture. It became known as Svabia on the Danube. Its inhabitants were mostly bilingual, speaking Hungarian and German.

Mihály Kilczer was from a hard working family of Temesgyarmata (Giarmata). He was the first of his family to attend a university.

Legend has it that his father's supervisor came up with some mathematical problems, and young Mihály solved them. So, the gentleman offered to educate him. He went to the gymnasium in Temesvár (Timosiara) and to the University of Selmec, from which he graduated with honors. Among the few treasures my mother saved when we fled during the war were a silver cigarette case, adorned with his monogram in diamond chips, and a silver pocket watch, both prizes he won upon graduation.

My father loved the university and he loved learning. He did that all his life. He also enjoyed remembering stories from his student years, and sang *"Gaudeanus Igitur"* with great vigor.

When he met my mother, she was seventeen years old, in finishing school. He was twenty-seven, the youngest director of the coal mines of Vajdahunyad (Hunadora). Had my mother been living with her title-conscious mother, this union never would have happened. However, my grandfather, Köváry Ernö, was a well-educated, open-minded man. He respected my father for his intellect and his ethics. He gladly gave his blessings. And Aunt Gizi, mother's stern aunt who raised her, was overjoyed that mother had found a husband, even if she was not blond and blue-eyed, as her pretty Kitty sister.

All was wonderful until 1920. After World War I, Transylvania became Romania, and the mines in Vajdahunyad closed. My father felt it his duty to return to Hungary what was theirs. My parents moved to Budapest, and began their nomadic existence, until they settled in Szentes.

I adored my father. I never heard him raise his voice. He treated the servants as he treated a princess. Our house was filled with books, and classical music, and flowers. He loved mother's beautiful dinner parties and enjoyed their guests; usually he did so quietly, but sometimes was forthcoming with *bon mots*. Everybody loved him.

None more than me.

His Saturdays were mine as well. After lunch we walked downtown. People passed us smiling at the perfectly dressed, graying gentleman, with

*My father*

a red-headed little girl, in deep conversation. Every Saturday we went to the bookstore, and I never left empty handed. Our second stop was the sweet shop, where I learned to eat enormous marzipan apples, filled with the most delicious chocolate filling.

On Sundays he and I went to the Catholic Church, mother to the Presbyterian. After the mass, we met mother and their friends at the hotel. I was fascinated by their conversations.

As the years went by, the conversations became more serious, and sad. War was closing in on us. We covered our windows with dark curtains, so airplanes would not see the lighted houses. Stores began to be empty; food was bought in smaller amounts via tickets. Our helpers, except a housekeeper, left to return to their families, their villages. My parents stayed up late, listening to the BBC news on the radio.

In 1940 I went to boarding school in Budapest, the *Erzsébet Nöiskola*, named after Hungary's beloved queen Elizabeth. I loved the school, and especially adored our well-known uniforms, the red aprons, as well as my friends from every corner of Hungary. I loved being in Budapest. My parents would come to visit on weekends, and during these visits Gerbeaud and the New York Café became our favorite stops, serving glorious *dobos torta,* which is a six-layered chocolate torte.

Still the war was getting closer and closer. By my third year at the Erzsébet, my parents kept me from going to school in Budapest. Airplanes were appearing much more, and other scary things were happening. Hitler's name was on everybody's mind, and even though Hungary was Germany's partner in this war, his way of ruling was not like ours. Our Regent Miklos Horthy's son died a strange death. It was whispered that the Nazis killed him, whispered very, very quietly. He had loved America, where he spent a year at Ford's factory, learning. Then on a sunny summer day, our Regent was invited for a conference in Germany, and while he was there, German paratroopers took over Hungary.

The Germans were everywhere. They were at our door, also, two officers, "requesting" a room for them. We were lucky, as in some cases they took whole houses. Our housekeeper saw guns in their room when she cleaned.

That was when my father had the first, very stern talk with me. I was told to watch every word I spoke, and to stay out of the officers' way. Of course my parents' nightly British news radio news were over, too. The silence was scary.

The talk then began to be of the end of the war. Yet the possibility of the Soviets taking over Hungary after the Germans was even more scary. My father assured us that since he never had anything to do with politics, we would be fine.

On November 4, 1944, the Margit Bridge was blown up in Budapest.

The more stories my father heard in secret conversations in his club, with friends, and with visiting Hungarian officers, the quieter my wonderful but rather naïve father got. Horror stories of the possible Soviet occupation left him with few words.

In mid-November 1944, my father decided that my mother and I should take up Aunt Pálma's invitation to join her family in Celldömölk, to the west of us and closer to the Austrian border.

By then we could actually hear the war approaching, as it grew louder and almost nonstop, it was so close to Szentes.

We packed quickly, and he put us on the train. There was not too much time for thinking. The trains were packed with people, who like us, wanted to be away from the sounds of war, and the war itself.

Father watched us board the train. He could not go, he said, he could not leave his office.

It was the most difficult day in my fourteen years. The train began slowly to move. I saw my father standing alone at the train station, with tears running down his face.

I had never seen him cry before.

## no name day for pálma

**AN INTERESTING TRADITION** in Hungary, and some other European countries, is the Name Day. It originated with the Christian calendar of Saints. It is, even to this day, celebrated there as we celebrate birthdays.

My mother's best friend's name was Pálma. She was my beloved *Pálma néni,* Aunt Pálma.

A name evidently not listed in the Christian calendar of Saints, because Aunt Pálma did not have a Name Day.

This was not the only interesting thing about her. She was brilliant. She quoted Goethe and Villon in four languages, among many other poets. Her library was filled with an enormous number of interesting books, she loved classical music as much as my mother, and she was beautiful. (As was my mother.)

She was fun too. One Fasching (the November 11th celebration just days before the commencement of Lent), my parents had a masked ball party. All the ladies came as beautiful princesses and regal queens. Beautiful Aunt Palma arrived on the arm of her husband, Uncle Ali, who was a dashing husar. Palma, however was NOT a princess, or queen. She came costumed as "Popeye, the Sailor Man."

Aunt Pálma shared her home with Uncle Ali, who was an officer and director of *Neptelekek* (Royal Hungarian horse farms), and their children, Alice and Peter. They were also beautiful, and much more. They rode horses since birth, and were brave, and strong, and everything, I, the sheltered only child, was not.

Still, they were our best friends.

By December 1944, I overheard a grown-up say, "The Germans are losing the war, and everybody knows that except Hitler."

The Hungarians made one more try to join the allied forces, but it was too late. The Soviets were getting closer and closer to Hungary's center. As were the stories of their behavior, about how the vodka was flowing, books were burned, and the outcry was heard: "hide your women" from being raped.

So after many phone conversations with Aunt Pálma, my father, who was still in the Western part of Hungary (Dunantul a.k.a. Transdanubia), accepted her generous invitation to my mother and me to travel to their home in Celldömölk, and stay for a while until things simmered down.

Again we underwent rapid packing, no time to say goodbye, even to our best friends, no time for tears, just off to the train station we went...

It was a bittersweet train ride. The journey was long, and we were mostly standing, back to back, pushed and pulled, as the overly filled train moved slower than usual. Babies, grandparents, elegant ladies, and sweet country women, heads wrapped in their babushes, all shared the same goal, to get as far from the war as possible.

It was wonderful to arrive in Celldömölk and see Aunt Pálma waiting for us with a carriage led by beautiful, noble Hungarian horses, and a perfectly suited coachman.

We were the last guests to arrive. Pálma's house was filled with relatives and friends. She gathered us around her. Her husband, Uncle Ali, was off fighting on the Soviet front. All in all, there were nine mothers, and nine children, ages three to fourteen years, in the house. I had just turned fourteen in October. Alice and I were the oldest.

Aunt Pálma was an amazing hostess. Magically, meals were served, beds were fitted and pillowed, and somehow she kept the mother guests, if not happy, somewhat contented, as much as it was possible.

We, the children, were gifted with two playrooms, which we named goreny tanya (polecat farms). Here we played games, painted, made toys, and enjoyed playing with the small kids. We only left for meals and to visit Aunt Pálma's salon in the afternoons, to listen to her read poems, and stories that brought important culture into our lives.

We the children, even us "older" ones, had little idea just how serious the war was. How our worlds would never be the same, and that we were living in the end of a war later named World War II. For most of us, we were losing our country and all of our belongings. Never to see our homes, our ancestors' lovely large portraits, our books, our monogramed family silver, our everything—not to mention our country, our way of life, ever again.

We had no idea that we had become refugees. We did not know about the brutality that took place all around us, the unimaginable use of other trains in our world.

On a gray December day, we, the children, were told to close our "polecat farms," help our mothers pack the suitcases, bundle up as warmly as possible, and be ready for yet another train ride, through Austria to the German *Albs* (in English, the Alps) to wait for American forces and the end of the war.

En route, we began to understand what war was.

The train stopped several times, rough and unexpected, throwing people and luggage hither and yon. Airplanes flew above us as we were herded out of the train, and ordered to lay against the embankment, very still, not moving, so we would not provide targets for the planes. Some of the planes dived down, scaringly, with gunfire thundering around us.

It was very difficult for the small children AND for us too.

Our hearts went out to the horses—eighty horses, Hungary's pride studs, were on the train behind us. Hearing the planes roar, they were as afraid as we were; their cries filled the planes and hills around us. It was a miracle that we survived…us humans and the beautiful horses. We were grateful, as we wiped the tears from our eyes, and could not speak, just said a quiet prayer.

**IT WAS CHRISTMAS EVE 1944** when we arrived at our destination.

The train stopped at a snow-covered hill, and above us, on top of a hill was a castle.

Our Christmas gift?

Not quite...

Aunt Pálma was greeted by a lady, who led us up to the castle.

We were in Gomadingeen, in the *Schwabische Albs.*

The train, still with the horses, went a bit further. The village Marbach had stables waiting for the Hungarian horses, where they could wait until (hopefully) American troops would find them. The Hungarian soldiers, who were taking care of the horses, had places to stay in Marbach as well.

We, the nine mothers and nine children, followed Aunt Pálma and her leading lady and climbed to the third floor of the building, finding two rooms: one large, dormitory style with nine beds, and a smaller one, for Aunt Pálma's few pieces of furniture that she was able to bring with us.

The lady told us a bit about the castle. It obviously had seen better days. Built in 1556 by Duke Carl Eugen, it had lived many lives. In 1929, a Samaritan Foundation used it as a hospice for invalids.

We had no idea where we were when we arrived...we only saw snow-covered, beautiful hills. We'd landed somewhere in the *Schwabische Albs,* Germany.

Forever positive, Pálma took a look at our new living quarters and declared, in German, *"Aber die Gegend ist wunderschön"* (but the region is beautiful).

Which became our cry, whenever somebody dared to complain.

The mothers cooked our meals, washed our clothes, read to us, and tried to smile. We, the children, roamed in the woods, skied down the hills on borrowed skis, and enjoyed our newly found freedom. Our mothers were in a different state of mind. Without newspapers or radio news, totally secluded from the war, and the world, they worried. We, the children, did not grasp the full enormity of the situation. Only when the sobbing of our mothers, heard in the dark *Schwabische* nights woke us, did we wonder about the reality.

Not having any news from my father, my mother became physically ill. Her slightly gray hair, piled in a pompadour, where she hid her jewelry, seemed more gray, day by day. Her famous *joie de vivre* also vanished. I was not much help. I loved the mountains, and for me, an only child, the companionship of eight other kids was most welcome.

I hugged her every morning, and copying Aunt Pálma, I assured her, *"Aber die Gegend ist wunderschön"* (but the region is beautiful).

\* \* \*

Spring 1945 arrived, the snow of the *Schwabische Alb* melted. The hills changed from white to spring green, and the perfume of lovely purple bushes lingered in the air. News was heard, every once in a while, from lonely, hungry soldiers, knocking on our doors, and with whom our mothers always shared a bowl of soup, or whatever meager food they had on hand.

One sunny spring day, we, the children, were playing in the front yard, when a bent, elderly man appeared at the end of the path.

"Another beggar," opined one of us, looking at the man, in ripped clothing, white beard, worn face, quietly surveying our little band. It took us both, the visitor and me a few minutes, before recognition...

I screamed, "Father!" and ran into his arms.

He had been walking for two weeks, stopping at farmhouses, asking for food, resting in sheds and stables along the way. His Hungarian money was not worth a cent, and mother had the jewelry. The food he carried was long gone. He left Budapest after the Soviet siege, and began to search for us.

Mother, incredulous, rose from her sickbed, and became her old self. They found a little room, and we were a family again.

A family, having lost all worldly goods, but we were alive!

By spring of 1945 the war became more audible, closer, even in the *Albs*. The sounds of war were numbing and frightening. The adults decided that we should await the possible fighting in the cellar.

After a couple of days we were running out of food. Mother volunteered to go up to the third floor to bring down some food. Some of the "old" kids, like me, went with her to help. While mother gathered food, we stood by the windows, and all at once, the murmuring war noise became heavy, a scary grumble, and at the end of the road there appeared a huge, roaring monster, followed by other huge monsters, *tanks.*

By the time we got to the front door, these tanks were lined up, facing the building with guns pointing to the door and windows. And we were face to face with soldiers in khaki uniforms and yellow neck scarves, pointing real guns at us.

As the rest of our group appeared from the cellar, we were lined up single row in front of the tanks. I will forever remember that afternoon, and how fright turned into smiles...

They were Americans.

Aunt Pálma spoke English, and she told them our story: we were Hungarian refugees, fleeing from the Soviets.

The commanding officer was from a place called "Texas," and his wife was of Hungarian descent... and, and, and...their soldiers were wonderful Americans.

So, toward the end of World War II, between the *Schwabiche Albs,* two worlds collided in a most peaceful fashion. It was our first encounter with smiling soldiers, long forgotten chocolates, and cookies. And from them we learned that chewing gum was not to be swallowed.

Surrounded by German hills, in front of huge American machines of war, we lost Hungarians amazingly felt a miracle happening because of the kindness of those nameless young American soldiers.

The rumble of the tanks, as they disappeared down the road, made us sad. Our face to face meeting with WAR was so different from the nightmare stories we had heard of the Soviet occupation.

As they drove away in their tanks, we said a prayer for the safety of these young American soldiers. They left us better than they found us.

They left strange boxes, filled with unfamiliar foods, much appreciated, as our supplies were diminishing.

They also left a large "OFF LIMITS" sign for the door, a sign that they had been here and that they had conquered this bit of the world.

I had such grateful feeling for this castle. There I got my father back, and all of us, mothers and children, felt safer. Even in our lost weeks there, we were alive, and the war, even as war, was kind to us.

Many years later I revisited the castle with my husband and mother-in-law. It was again an asylum for invalids. Visiting my German friends from the *Englisches Institut*, we also visited the castle. My friends had never heard of it, and wanted to see where I spent part of the war.

It was not until I was eighty years old, that I learned that Grafeneck had, during 1940, been used by the Nazis as the first euthanasia center for mentally and physically disabled people.

Long before I was there, or my mother or father, or the other refugees, or the Americans…

I carry the horror of this knowledge forever.

## french grace in war

**WE WERE NAIVE ENOUGH** to think that we were done with our "war" experience, based on how easy and nice it was with the Americans. But somewhere, far away, the allied forces were meeting, studying their maps, and deciding on how the countries that *lost* the war would be taken care of, and who would get what.

"Don't unpack your suitcases, Hungarian friends."

Hungary was the gift to the Soviets, with very little hope that the Soviets would be gone soon. Parts of Germany went that way too. Baden and Wurttenberg were split. The north zone became American, the South became French.

By April 30, 1945, all these occupation rules were to be done.

And they were done.

We were now under French occupation.

My parents were Frankophiles and delighted …a little too soon. The French soldiers were unfriendly, and somewhat rough. And they were tired, they wanted the job done and over with. There were no chocolate and chewing gum gifts for the children.

These men had had enough of war. Their memories of the German occupation were too vivid, too hurtful, and too recent.

Understandable.

So they went through our stuff. They especially liked our boots and our cameras. Without a smile, they looked for rings on fingers and necklaces. My mother still had her jewelry in her bouffant hair. But what she had in a suitcase in a large box was an even more cherished part of her history, and the only one she was able to bring with her, the Kövary flat-silver. Some pieces went back five-hundred years, having been passed down from generation to generation, monogrammed, with the crown above the monograms. There were a few other silver pieces as well.

The young French soldier's eyes became quite large as he opened the box. Then he went looking for his officer. "Come, come see," he said.

And the officer liked what he saw too and began to close the box, holding it as if it were already his. Mother, without a moment of fright, but with tears running down her face, reached for the box. In perfect French, she told the officer that we were Hungarian refugees, and most of this silver was old, old family pieces, and it was the only thing she was able to bring with her in a suitcase.

He did not answer. He just put the box on a table, opened it, and began to make two piles. One were the pieces with the monogram, the other without. When he was done, he put the pieces without the monogram in the box, looked at mother, and pointing to the monogramed pile, and without a word, started to walk away with the box.

We just stood there, we could not move. Mother reached out to shake his hand, barely able to say her thanks.

Another World War II miracle.

I own this silver now, in a very special wooden box. I cherish this silver, these few but so special mementos of my heritage. And I take good care of it.

I don't polish them every Thursday, as I did as a child in Szentes when I sneaked out to the

*Saved by the French*

forbidden kitchen, when mother left the house, to "help" our staff to polish the silver.

But when I polish them to keep them shiny, I remember and I realize how fortunate I AM. And, my children, the next generation, and my grandsons, the future, possibly will understand too.

\*  \*  \*

As the French soldiers left, we were given twenty-four hours to get out of the place. Uncle Ali, who had arrived from prisoner of war camp, and my father found an empty inn in a nearby village.

We gathered our things and slept there on the floor. In a couple days they found some empty barracks, with cots, another "home." We felt like nomads, moving from place to place. These were unpleasant, sad, scary days, but we were still alive.

*"Aber die Gegend ist wunderschon..."*

The region was still beautiful.

Aunt Pálma and her family were packing up and moving to Munich, where they had friends.

Father walked from village to village, looking for the Bürgermeisters (mayors) in hopes of finding a place to live. And miracle of miracles, the mayor of Gomadingen had two rooms, in his house. This was a *huge* step in our lives. Father went to a nearby town. When he got back the hair on mother's head was missing a couple rings, but we had a HOME!

A palace could not have made my mother happier. A tiny room on the first floor was mine, a larger one upstairs was my parents'. We shared the kitchen and the bathroom. The house was immaculate. Mr. Bürgermeister was quiet and sweet, a wonderful man. Mrs. Bürgermeister was ample and matter of fact. They were simple country people with hearts of gold. Slowly word got out in the village that mother could sew. Hesitantly at first, the women in the village began to bring clothing to be re-made to mother since fabrics were still not avaliable. They paid for her services with freshly baked bread, eggs, potatoes and fruits. This was most welcome, since food was sparse.

And it was much better than trading diamonds for potatoes, just to stay alive.

Frau Bürgermeister adored mother. As time went by, we met some Hungarians in the neighborhood, and she noticed that mother used the familiar "Du" in conversation, as was the Hungarian custom with friends within the same social standing. One day Frau Bürgermeister asked my mother why she used "Du" with her friends, and the formal "Sie" with her.

Mother did not want to explain to Mrs. B about the Hungarian upper classes' social customs and hurt her feelings, so she just told her that we used the "Du" with friends.

"Well, are we not friends?" inquired Mrs. B.

From then on, it was Luisa, and Martha, good friends using the Du.

Mother was teary, and considered this the loveliest compliment from a simple, wonderful German farmwife to a titled Hungarian woman.

Indeed they were our friends, our saviors, forever cherished in our grateful memories.

# juhász gyula's poem

*Milyen volt szökesége, nem tudom már*
*De azt tudom hogy szökék a mezők*
*Ha dus kalásszal jön a sárguló nyár*
*S e szökeségben ujra érzem öt....*

Google translation:

What was his habit, I do not know
But I know what the fields are
if you have a rush with the
sargulo summer
And I usually rush back

My translation:

I have forgotten just
How golden blond he was,
But still know in the
Sun-bathed meadows,
Summers yellowing
Pale blond grass,
In the fields' blondness
I feel his soul, alas....

Forgive me, Juhász Gyula...
It is one of my favorite poems.

His name was Andris...
And I loved him.

## hopeless no more

**TIME PASSED.** By Christmas 1945 we even had a Christmas tree in our tiny habitat in the Albs. Mother made ornaments from scraps of paper. Father continued his adventurous walks around the neighborhood villages. Whereas some of our friends were busy in black market activities, he made friends with the villagers, and in turn they helped him. Right before Christmas he arrived home with a huge Cheshire cat smile on his face, and a large package under his arm. He had found a gift for mother—an ancient, foot-pedaled sewing machine. After a few days of tinkering he had the machine in working order.

Mother was the happiest refugee in the neighborhood and became an official seamstress.

My father often came home with scraps of wires and other strange-looking metal things. These he cleaned meticulously, and laid out on his table. These became, one fine day, a portable pocket radio, his very own invention. Unfortunately, he was unable to sell it.

Everybody was happy…well, as happy as possible under the circumstances.

Except me.

There were no high schools around. I had nice friends, my age, who walked down the hill to get milk with me at "The Moltke" and Mr. and Mrs. Bürgermeister were glad that Hans, the wealthiest farmer's son, joined our little group. They thought that this pointed to a very good future for me. However, my Cinderella dreams were not quite of the *Albs,* no matter how *schön die Gegend war* (how beautiful the region was).

Father was telling me stories of Universities in Paris and Budapest, which felt almost impossible for me to imagine. At age fourteen, I felt my future was very dark.

Mother's best friend, the Baroness von Maltzahn, often came for tea. Well, not quite the kind of tea Mother's staff would have served on Herend porcelain, but refugee tea, spiced with wonderful stories of operas, great books, Budapest, Paris, and Baroness von Maltzahn's castle in Germany.

On a lovely early September day in 1945, a month before my fifteenth birthday, she was smiling and full of news. The boarding school she'd attended many years ago on the wonderful island on the Bodensee, in Lindau, had just reopened.

"Isn't that just *fabelhaft?*" the Baroness said, indicating it would be even more fabelhaft if I, as in daughter Márta, could go there.

Since I knew that was impossible, I left their tea party and reached for my handkerchief in my little room. However, mother and Liselotte, the Baroness von Maltzahn, worked quickly. She telephoned the Englisches Institut, made an appointment for Mother and me, even though the school year had already started and the enrollment was full.

"Could we just come to visit?" pleaded Mother. We could and we did. The next day.

Stepping off of the train to Lindau, we walked to the *Englisches Institut*. We waited in the Mater Oberin's little waiting room until the magical door opened, and then we walked into her office of the Mother Superior.

Mother began with our story. And she was brilliant.

My gentle, lovely mother could be a veritable tigress when it came to me.

The Mater Oberin, a slim, slight and rather stern nun, looked us over, her glasses pushed on her elegant nose as she listened to Mother's story, rather matter of factly. *Mater Oberin* smiled, as she understood and was very, very sorry, but there was no room for another student. Former students' daughters, legacies, have been waiting for a long time for the Institut to reopen, she said, and there was indeed a long waiting list.

I still remember that moment, as if it were yesterday. Gone was my sophistication, my grown-up demeanor, and months of self control. I sat there, facing *Mater* Maria Furtenbach, totally dissolved in tears, and very embarrassed.

"Maybe next year," Mother said soothingly, thanking *Mater Oberin* for the interview, trying to get me out of the chair facing *Mater Oberin*, who looked up, above her glasses, and shook my hand goodbye.

"Just in case of a very slight possibility of a cancellation and a student spot opening up," she said, "the number for your clothes, and all your belongings would be 24."

Two days after we got home to Gomadingen, a boy on his bicycle delivered a telegram for me from the *Englisches Institut* in Lindau in Bodensee from Mater Maria Furtenbach, the *Oberin* of the *Englisches Institut*.

It read, "We have an opening, please come as soon as possible."

And two days later, I was a student again.

*The beautiful, small island of Lindau in the Bodensee*

# love, love, love lindau

**LINDAU** in in Bodensee in Bavaria, Germany, changed my life.

Just remembering is joy and gratitude. Not before, nor since, did I love a school as much as the *Englisches Institute* in Lindau in Bodensee.

It really IS in Bodensee, a tiny island, almost bordering with Austria and Switzerland, truly a beautiful wonderland. Snowcovered *Albs* faced the island; boats glided into the harbor, waving to the sculpture of a smiling lion; and in the midst of this lovely little fairytale world, in the blessed year of 1945, was reborn the *Madchen Middleschule*, the *Englisches Institut* (a girls' middle school).

It had been a Catholic high school (and boarding school), founded by the English Maria Ward, and was known as the "Ladies of Loretto." The school was acknowledged worldwide for its education of young women. In Budapest, the school was the most excellent one for *"Angol kisasszonyok"* (English young ladies). It had closed at beginning of the Nazi party's rule. The nuns, *Maters* and Sisters, scattered and hid all over Germany, and the Nazis took over the buildings.

The reopening of the school in Lindau in 1945, at the end of World War II, was somewhat of a miracle. One by one, the Sisters, magically finding and putting on their habits, returned to their "Mother home" in Lindau. Which they found totally trashed, almost ruined, but still standing—the *Englisches Institut*.

PhD *Mater* professors, Sister chefs, Sister nurses, cleaning Sisters—all rolled up their blessed sleeves. In nearly six months, the school was painted, the Chapel had its cross back, kitchens were finished, beds for the boarding students were topped with with soft German featherbeds, classrooms once again had black boards and desks, and Sisters were happily waiting for students.

One by one we arrived. I, with my #24 proudly displayed, came a week late and as an Auslanderin (a foreigner), yet was welcomed as lovingly as the other girls.

All of us—the *Maters,* the Sisters of the order of Maria Ward, and both day students and boarding students—united in one joyous, energized, wondrous goal: To recreate the school, to teach, to learn…to try to forget the war, and to look forward to a happier future.

We never heard the nuns complained. We heard them pray.

The only thing we did *not* have were books. When it came to books, the change from the Nazi-world to the post-war world was a longer process. We took notes in our classes, happily so. Mater Hermenegild taught math (and I still loved her...); tiny, sweet *Mater* Melanie taught French; *Mater* Angela oversaw our dormitories; *Mater* Barbara the kitchen; and *Fraulein* Schiller taught gym and household subjects.

No radio, no TV, no computers in those long-ago days.

Just wonderful people!

We wrote and performed plays. Girls who studied musical instruments gave concerts. We wrote gently humorous poems about our professsors (they loved them). Our *Bunte Abends* (colorful evenings) were a mish-mash of performances and became somewhat legendary.

There was talent all over the place. Marion Lohaus from Düsseldorf was brilliant; the other Marion, talented and sweet (her daughter Petra is my friend on Facebook); Inge and Ellen, both from nearby regions, so wonderful. And all, like Inge, whose family owned a mill and thus received more food packages, shared them with us, with delight.

More than anything, we laughed a lot in Lindau. Looking back, it seems to make sense. The war was over and we were still alive, and we appreciated our learning opportunities. The nuns' joy pointed us to a future. Food was still scarce, but the Sisters created miracles with our food rations. We did not have a lot of clothes. I, the refugee, thanks to my mother's creativity, had probably more than the other girls. We shared things. In our graduating photo, four girls wear my dresses, and nobody knew that my winter coat was originally a blanket, dyed brown, and my favorite outfit was made by my mother from an orange-dyed bedspread. The shops were still empty.

How my parents got me through the three years in Lindau, I'll never know. Bless them, the nuns must have had something to do with it, and one of mother's large diamonds was no longer around. And she worked very hard on that old, old Singer machine.

I remain so grateful.

As all things come to an end, so did our years at the *Englisches Institut*. My final exams were done. I graduated and did pretty well, almost even in math. My parents were pleased and father was especially pleased, since I was speaking High German again. It was the least I could do for them, for all their sacrifices.

I still consider my three years there some of the happiest in my life. I owed *Mater* Maria Furtenback, the *Mater Oberin*, my life and my future.

She was known to be stern, but always fair, and in me she found a lifelong supporter and friend. I adored her, loved every nun, every student, every nook and cranny, every chair, the chapel, everything in that school. I became the class clown, laughing, singing, studing, and playing my way through the *Englisches Institut*.

I visited *Mater* Maria with Bill Blades in her retirement. I went to our 50th reunion with all our friends.

And I'll never forget anything about Lindau.

Especially *Mater* Maria, who became my best friend, as an adult, through beautifully written letters, and remained my friend, and champion, until the day she died.

## DECEMBER 30, 1948.

An unforgettable day.

Marked in my journal: "The future seems unforeseeable, and oblique...."

I lost my father.

My mother and I had been taking the train to Tübingen every day. He was at the University Hospital. Cancer. He was sixty-one years old.

Up to the last minute, he worked on one of the wonderful projects that were such a part of his life and that he felt would make the world a better place to live in.

A magical, amazing, joyful, loving, brilliant human being he was, my father.

The only thing he could not understand was why I was always, in every school, on the border of flunking mathematics. No matter how I tried.

Our friends gathered around my mother and me. They came from Reutlingen, Gomadingen, Münich, and other places. There were Hungarians, Germans, and French friends, and as a result a lovely mix of languages, stories, and tears. Most importantly, mother's best friends, Aunt Pálma and Liselotte von Maltzan, were there.

Along with the roses, a handful of Hungarian earth covered his casket. I still do not know where it came from.

A German priest and a Hungarian author gave the eulogies, and the funeral was followed by a beautiful reception.

\* \* \*

Even though I do not cherish today's technology, I am unbelievably grateful to Google.

Seventy years after that sad day in that sad little German cemetery, I still find lectures my father gave, articles he wrote, and groups he was a member of, on my computer.

*Köszönöm,* Papa.

And *thank you,* Google.

# and then there were two

*Once valuable Hungarian currency*

**AND THEN** there were two....

Just the two of us, my mother and I. Still in the midst of grief, I had the feeling that from some glorious cloud in heaven, my father was looking down on us, and taking care of us.

Miracles *do* happen… we were moving, my mother and I, from our beloved hills and village to a real city…a CITY!

Reutlingen.

It was not a major move, just two suitcases for each of us, a sewing machine, and a box. A sizeable box, filled with beautiful but by now totally worthless *pengös* (Hungarian money). A few months earlier, these *pengös* could have been useful for buying wonderful, or needed things in Hungary.

In our last minutes before we became refugees, we emptied 10s, 20s, 50s, 100s, even a bunch of glorious 1000 banknotes from our bank into the box. Amazing, how things change. *Pengös* in Hungary became *forints*, and I imagine that even banks were in Soviet hands by now.

Still, my mother was determined to seriously and strongly hold on to the box that was part of our past.

"Maybe someday, they will be good again", she said, "or we will wallpaper our powder room with them."

Powder room?

We were en route to an "apartment," two tiny rented rooms for our new lives in Reutlingen, and we were feeling lucky to look forward to them.

Amazing things do happen. Somewhere, someone knew of my mother. The magical "sewing lady" was becoming known in the *Alb's* villages. The word was that she was talented, could even make wedding dresses tastefully. *And*, she was nice.

The firm Heinzelman was known for manufacturing swimsuits in Reutlingen. At the war's end, they became interested in making women's dresses, and were looking for a directrice for their new department. Somehow they had heard of my mother.

"Would Madame Kilczer be interested in having an interview with one of the owners, Herr Hans Heizelman?" they asked in a letter.

Oh, yes, Madame was. And she was hired.

"When could she start?"

"Right away," answered Mother.

They were lovely people, Herr and Frau Heizelman. Mother fit into their world well. They loved art, and had a well-chosen art collection, and the time had arrived when they needed their collection cataloged.

Well, it just so happened that Madame Kilczer had a daughter, who had just finished high school, was wild on the typewriter, and *loved* art.

Yes. I was hired.

I had an "office" in the corner of a beautiful large space filled with paintings, called *Ritter Saal* (Knight Hall), where I began learning impossible-to-spell artists' names, and answering letters to galleries, and loving the whole picture.

I even got a salary. I was paid with real German money. All this within walking distance to our tiny "home."

There was a sizeable group of Hungarians in Reutlingen. Word got around that we were there, and they opened their hearts and houses to us. Our home was pretty open, also. Mother had the teapot full, and our lives became somewhat normal.

Normal?

Well, not quite normal, but better.

Mother was getting used to her 9:00-6:00 world, was meeting more and more friends, and playing bridge. I joined a Hungarian student club and became Germany's representative of the Hungarian student newspaper *Ahogy Lehet (How Possible)*, printed in Paris.

Along the way I filled out an application to the Catholic Displaced and Refugee Students sponsored by the Relief Department of Pax Romana, Switzerland, for a scholarship to a college in the blessed *United States of America*.

And somehow, I sort of forgot about that application.

Somehow, I fell, and I fell pretty well. In love.

He was everything. Endre, a Hungrian author, was well read, spoke not just Hungarian and German, but French and English, loved the theatre and *good* movies, was a perfect gentleman who kissed a lady's hands, and was ten years older than I.

And even though he called me "child," he loved me too.

We read books together, we went to *good* movies, and we looked to the moon, walking hand in hand. My mother liked him and his family, and they liked us.

I was in heaven.

Until on a stormy October day, when our sweet postman handed me a very business-like envelope from the Catholic Displaced and Refugee Students. The letter was happy to inform me that I was the recipient of a four-year scholarship to:

*Marian College, Indianapolis, Indiana, the United States of America*

A few months earlier I would have done a *csardas* dance on the village square from joy. But that was pre Endre, and moonlight, and love.

"I am NOT going!" I cried to my mother.

"Oh, yes, you are…it is your FUTURE!" she replied.

"I will NOT stand in your way, YES, you are going," said Endre.

There was a not a dry handkerchief left in my life (I did not know of Kleenex then).

So I began to pack. The brown dyed blanket that Mother had turned into a coat would work for the cold Indiana winters. She also had made me long skirts, just introduced as the fashion in Paris, and bought me a new suitcase.

But when the time came to leave for the train to a Camp called "Grohn," where displaced persons gathered to wait for their ships to the United States, she did not come with me to the station. She hugged me and put a cross with her finger on my forehead for blessing.

Neither of us could speak.

Endre practically pushed me onto the train...

All alone, towards a brand new world.

## camping at grohn

**ON NOVEMBER 7, 1949,** in my brown coat made out of a blanket, and my orange outfit made out of a bedspread, I boarded the train in Reutlingen, headed for Camp Grohn, in northern Germany. I waved good bye to Endre and Laci, my friends who accompanied me to the train station. The good bye from my mother at our tiny apartment had been very, very difficult.

But I was on my way, on the first step toward the greatest adventure of my life.

Lonely, scared, but somehow free, and hopeful. And very grateful.

Our destination was Camp Grohn, North Bremen, outside of Bremerhafen. Since 1945, Camp Grohn had been a relocation camp for displaced persons in all of Europe. By November 1945, over a million people had been relocated from there by American forces through the International Refugee Orgnization. Another five and a half million would travel through Bremen-Grohn before the camp closed in 1954.

I was one of those millions of fortunate ones.

Buses took us from the train station to the barracks at Grohn. Everything was very well organized. We were given our barrack assignments, our numbers and maps. We were informed of our dining assignments. In every barrack there was a bulletin board, advising the residents of their ship and sailing dates. This bulletin board became our bible. Several times a day we would stand before it, searching for our names.

As well as everything was organized, two weeks at Grohn seemed an eternity. We were able to receive mail, which was nice. Most people were accompanied by their families. There were a few students alone, who also had scholarships in America. Actually, we students were fortunate because we were whisked through faster.

Food was plenty (magically, surprisingly) and good. Friendly, smiling American faces were everywhere. They showed American movies. The Red Cross gifted us with little care packages filled with fine smelling soaps and shampoos, things we had not seen since the beginning of the war. I met some lovely Hungarian families, who were kind enough to "adopt" a lonely stranger, me. We played bridge, exchanged stories of our pasts, and even found mutual friends.

Still, not finding one's name on the bulletin board day by day was disheartening.

I worried about my mother, left alone in Reutlingen, even though I received an encouraging letter, typical of her kindness and love, which reached me before I sailed.

I missed everything familiar, everything so far away. My todays seemed like a dream, unreal.

Then a morning arrived when I was summoned for a last interview, in a very business-like office. Uniforms, even almost at the war's end, seemed frightening to me. But the officer, who sat behind a large desk, smiled and was friendly. Next to him was an interpreter, which was great, since my English was almost non-existent at the time.

He asked me fairly basic questions, about my home, my last school, my interests. He congratulated me on receiving a scholarship, and assured me that I would like studying in America. He was kind. He shared with me that he had a daughter about my age. He said she was a freshman, a term that I did not understand, who was also filled with anxiety about her first year in college.

Then he asked me, if I had any questions or worries.

"Yes, my mother," I answered.

I told him about losing my father recently, and that my mother was alone in Germany, that she applied for entry to the United States, but that could take a long, long time…many years sometimes.

He asked for the particulars about my mother's application and wrote everything down in a large book. Then he stood up, shook my hand, and said, "You will do fine."

Instead of waiting for months, or even years, when I arrived at Marian College, there was already a letter from my mother. She wrote me that magically, she was slated to travel to Grohn immediately, and a month after my arrival, she too sailed to the United States.

Another incredible angel had worked a miracle. It happened through a lovely American officer in Grohn, whom I met just for a few minutes, and whose name I did not even know, and whom I could not even thank, but who remained in our hearts and prayers.

## after the war

**ALL AROUND** us there were decaying mementoes of war.

The silhouettes of once proud buildings reduced to rubble were grim reminders of everything the people in line, waiting to board the ship, were desperately trying to forget. The sky was gray, the ocean was gray, the ship gently rocking by the shore was gray. I cast a giant slate-gray shadow in the mirror of the sea. The shadow seemed to extend itself and cover the people on the shore, they too seemed gray…gray and tired.

In Paris, Dior had just introduced the "new look," dropping fashionable women's skirts to mid-calf, the trend of which my mother had caught wind and enhanced my wardrobe. It was obvious that this news, which was rocking the fashion world facing another renaissance after the war, had had no effect on these people waiting in the shadow. Their clothes, just like the people, had seen better days. They stood in the long line, clutching their shabby coats tightly, shielding their bodies against the brisk November wind. Their faces seemed ashen beneath the ruddy masks painted on by the ocean breeze.

Yet, their eyes were alive.

I stood approximately in the middle of the waiting line, yet I almost felt as if I was just an observer.

"I wonder if the eyes really are a mirror of the soul," I mused to myself, as I looked down the line, trying to make eye contact with as many strangers in the crowd as I could. I had just turned nineteen a month ago, and thought myself terribly profound and philosophical. I tried to read their eyes, not realizing that what they mirrored were the exact emotions reflected in my own…I saw fear, apprehension, excitement, and perchance hope.

We were mostly East European refugees, gathered at Bremenhafen, Germany, on this windy November morning in 1949. After years, months of waiting, we were finally affixed with a small piece of paper, with just a number for a passport.

A small, but magical paper pinned to our coats, served as our passports to the United States of America.

"Number."

"Ja."

"Number."

"Da."

"Number."

"Igen."

It was my turn to point a hesitant finger, to show an officer my number tag. #856 was boarding the General C.C. Ballou. #856 was being given a chance for a new life, in a new, free world where #856 would, someday soon, be known by a name again.

The ship patiently swallowed the people, speaking in many tongues. The General C.C. Ballou was readying herself for yet another voyage across the ocean; she was once again becoming a floating babel filled with refugees. By 1949 she was a little tired, a little shopworn, having carried American troops back and forth during the war named World War II, and since the war's end, she carried DPs—displaced persons—searching for new homes. No one cared what she looked like. To us she was a symbol of hope, a symbol of new beginnings.

I was still incredulous. The line moved so smoothly and so rapidly. This final phase of my long, lonely journey was but a second in the seeming eternity that led me here. Although it had been only a couple of weeks, it seemed as if it had been years since I said goodbye to my mother in Reutlingen, as if I had been on the road forever, alone, getting ready for this very moment.

Now the waiting in two camps, waiting in food lines, waiting for shots, waiting to be interrogated, waiting for papers, waiting to see my name on a ship-boarding list, all faded into nothingness. No bells, no cannons heralded this big event. My heart pounded and I thought that everyone around me could hear it. My tears covered my face. I was sure that my legs would give way and instead of in America, I would end up either dead, or deadly embarrassed in the murky water below.

But I did not fall. I was on board.

By now, people were pushing and shoving. The inquires in many tongues were answered as best as they could be. Between interpreters and sign language, we all began to find our way toward our destinations. Mothers with babies and the elderly went first. Then we, the hearty souls, were plunged all the way to the sub-belly of the ship. The cabin, which was to become my home, and the home of my seventy-eight roommates for the next ten days, sported rows upon rows of three-tiered hanging bunks.

I felt grateful to my long ago gym teacher, whose drills enabled me now to crawl into a middle bunk more easily than some of my fellow travelers. I threw my bags on the bunk, very, very close to my body. For the next ten days I had a spot of my own in the world.

At half past four o'clock on November 15, 1949, the air became alive with roaring. The engines had spoken.

We were on our way.

The voices around me echoed the roaring. I could feel the excitement all around me. Haggard shoulders straightened, tired bodies awakened, and people were pushing, almost by instinct, finding their way through the narrow passages, up, up to the deck, for a final glimpse— to say goodbye, farewell to the common denominator for all these people embarked on this voyage.

We took a last look, and goodbye Europe....

Poles, Latviens, Lithuanians, Slavs, Chechs and Hungarians from all corners of Europe, all homeless, made so by what future historians would refer to simply as World War II, stood together. Maps would show different, changed boundaries, meaningless to future generations, yet within these boundaries, each and every person on this ship left a part of themselves. They left a country, a home, some land, and the worst, somebody they loved. Yet we were the fortunate ones, to have this opportunity. We had a number affixed to us, declaring the right to be here, leaning over the railing, waving good bye to huts, houses, and castles way beyond the German shoreline.

Shouts and cries filled the air.

*We are moving...we are actually moving*, I thought.

# on the ocean, in the c.c. ballou

**THE SQUIER CLASS** transport ship named General C.C. Ballou was born in 1945 for U.S. Navy transportation. She had wandered the world—Marseilles, Calcutta, Manila, Japan, Australia—before I met her.

History tells that from 1950 to 1952, she carried refugees from Europe to the United States of America.

Sorry to doubt "history."

I, as a refugee, boarded the C.C. Ballou in November 1949. According to my memories, I was 1,863 miles from Bremen, and 2,260 miles from New York on November 24, 1949, on the way to wonderland.

The first two days were glorious, exciting and good. We were led to our bunks, in large dormitory like spaces, in steerage. The three-tiered bunks slept about one hundred people per "stateroom." We had a list of our dining time and place. It took a whole day to find our way in our huge home on the ocean.

Everything seemed well planned and perfectly organized.

We were given jobs. I was assigned to the ship's newspaper, since I spoke German. I loved that, but I almost lost that job, and almost found myself cleaning bathrooms, the most unliked job of all jobs.

Some people were "bosses." I was told to stay out of their way. A young boss, wearing a blue baret, speaking a Slav language, seemed to be watching me. It was uncomfortable. I mentioned this to my adopted ship-family, and they were concerned. On the third day, Mr. Blue Beret approached me. In very poor German, he invited me to a birthday party at his cabin that evening. My "family" strongly advised me not to go, and made it their business to have somebody around me all the time. By the time the invitation was repeated several times, my naiveté dawned on me, and I was afraid of his punishment (cleaning bathrooms) for the rest of the voyage. But I still declined to go.

No need to have worried. About the fourth day on board, a winter storm approached. Dining tables turned upside down, dishes covered the floors, and everything and everybody was thrown side by side. The sea's power was magnificent and frightening. Soon the decks emptied, and the majority of the passengers took to their bunks, very, very seasick. I was cursing the day I ever wanted this journey, and did not leave my bunk for three days…miserable.

Finally somebody came around with Dramamine pills and suggested that fresh air would be the best medicine. Oranges were the only thing I could eat for the rest of the voyage, but misery was soon forgotten, as the ocean calmed down. We watched the mighty water turning blue and turquoise, smooth, and beautiful, as we sat wrapped in blankets on the deck.

On the eleventh night of our voyage, like a mirage and a miracle, the lights of New York appeared from afar, magnificently reflected in the dark waters. The next morning, oh, the next morning there she was, waiting for us: "the poor, the homeless, the huddled masses yearning to be free." The Lady of Hope, the Statue of Liberty. Our babel-like shouts greeted her, in many languages, as she stood there, with her lantern held high, welcoming us to our new home, our new world: America.

I had just turned nineteen.

Even now, so many, many years later, I still look at the Statue of Liberty when I am in New York and thank her for that magical welcome for a refugee…

Only, this time, as an American citizen.

# good morning, sweet liberty

**ON A SUNNY, LATE-FALL MORNING,** we arrived in New York City, in the United States of America. It was November 30, 1949.

I was so happy to be on *terra firma* again, and SO amazed to be in America.

Where everything was LARGE....

A large bus awaited us, to take us to the train station: the Grand Central Terminal.

And grand it is! Huge! At that time, 250,000 people commuted through it every day.

Among all these people, Red Cross ladies waited for us, the refugees, with coffee and cookies.

And, the ever-helpful people of the NCWC (National Catholic Welfare Council) waited to welcome us in the USA. Upon our arrival, they gave us each $3.00 and a welcoming hug.

The next step was to find our luggage. Again, amazingly organized, each piece of luggage was tagged according to our name's first letter.

Easy to find, under K I found my suitcases and porters helped to take them, and me, to a zoll station. Since they did not find anything "bad" in my luggage, I was taken to the NCWC area to wait.

A lovely Hungarian friend of mine, Paula, was in New York. She had arrived a few months ahead of me, since she had received a scholarship to Manhattanville College. She had sent me her phone number and promised to meet me in the city when I arrived in America.

I called her, and within an hour, there she was…very changed, very chic, very *American*. What a joy to see a friend!

And a city—large, large, large! Fifth Avenue was unbelievable!

After years of empty stores, it was astonishing to see every store (also huge) filled with beautiful things, all there for happy shoppers. I took in the sights of smiling people, a glorious cathedral, yellow cabs everywhere, and most women with carefully applied makeup, beautifully dressed, carrying bags filled with their just-bought goodies.

Paula had to ask me not to stare (yes, me, the "sophisticated" one). But I could not believe my eyes!

And for the first time in my grown-up life, with my $3.00, I purchased some nylon stockings in a drug store, and still had $2.00 left.

We "lunched" in New York City…oh, my !

Paula told me a lot about her college. She loved it. She had become almost fluent in English. She enjoyed the students, and the professors, and their help with her adjustment. The college, understanding a refugee's situation, also gave her $25.00 a month for her needs, and $100.00 a year for clothing.

Around 6:00 in the afternoon, she handed me a package of cookies and apples, took me back to Grand Central, and returned to Manhattanville. I will never forget her kindness to a newly arrived me. Again alone and lonely, I with my suitcases just sat and waited.

NCWC helpers were again helpful. They handed me my ticket and put me in a Pullman car of a shining train. They also informed a lovely, white-bearded porter of my situation, to make sure that I would not miss getting off the train in Indianapolis, Indiana, USA.

On December 1, 1949, at 11:00 a.m., I arrived in Indianapolis. A bit teary, I said goodbye to the very kind porter, who checked on me all through the train ride, and with whom I could talk, because once upon a time, he was a German refugee himself. As I shook his hand goodbye, he jumped back on the moving train, waved me goodbye and good luck..... and in my hand he had left a brand new $20.00 bill. Another helping angel I thank in my prayers.

In the train station at Indianapolis, Indiana, USA, stood a *Monsignor,* a Franciscan sister, the student body president, and a vice president of Marian College, with wonderful smiles, waiting for ME! They led me to an auto and drove me to my home-to-be, for the next four years. They were smiling and talking and although I did not understand much of their welcome greetings, I was very happy to see them, and duly grateful for their kindness and smiles. And so, my adventure began....

In America!

# marian college

**MARIAN COLLEGE** is now Marian University. It celebrated its seventy-fifth anniversary in 2012. Founded as a Catholic women's college, the school was run by Franciscan Sisters. In the most capable hands of its eighth president, Daniel J. Elsener, it has blossomed into one of Indiana's major universities.

I will always be grateful for the opportunities it gave me.

Still, the beginning was a little difficult.

In my journal, at the end of freshman year, I wrote, "Bittersweet, I am so tired, physically, and mentally...."

My very favorite thing (after years of sharing them with many people) was my beautiful, brand new, private pink bathroom. I was amazed by how pretty the girls were, how well dressed, how pretty their smiles, how beautiful the campus was, especially the art department, a building originally built as the home of a millionaire.

I worked hard on my English. I worked in the kitchen after breakfasts, lunches, and dinners, but not for pay. Unlike Manhattanville, Marian did not give us a stipend for clothes and other needs. My $23 gifts from the Red Cross and the train porter (which was $22 post my purchase of nylons) had to last until my mother arrived in America and had a job. At that point, I wondered what the other DP girls did.

The American girls were mostly from small Indiana towns, with little interest in Europe, or wars, or me. Some made fun of my English and tried to teach me bad English words...to say to the nuns.

I never knew if they laughed at me, or with me.

Most of them (*not* all...) just loved to count their cashmere sweaters.

I had interesting things happen, too. With the help of a dictionary (and the German professor), I wrote an article for the *Indiana Catholic and Record* about being a refugee. Somehow, it got in the hands of the NCWC and it was republished all over America. I received lovely letters and speaking invitations, and Marian College was pleased.

At one gathering at the public library, there were six speakers, all refugees from different countries. Some spoke only German and their own languages, and I tried to translate. There was a grumpy older gentleman who was not happy with anything in America and he shared this with the audience, in German. I tried to soften his unpleasant tirades, and translated accordingly.

From the audience, there was a lovely, heartfelt laughter.

At the end of it all, there came a couple who wanted to shake hands with me. They were Beth and Rudi Haerle, and the laughter came from Rudi, who spoke German, and understood what I was doing.

It felt as if a new world opened its door for me. They asked if they could take me for ice cream, and a lifelong friendship was born. They were intelligent, interesting, curious, and kind, kind people. They had two sons in college. Through the years, they treated me like family. They had a beautiful home, filled with art, which reminded me of home. They met Bill Blades, and liked him too. When I got married, I asked Rudi Harerle to walk me down the aisle, and when their first granddaughter (George Haerle's daughter) was born, she was the first brand new baby I ever saw. I felt safe with them. I don't know if they knew what an enormous change their friendship created for me.

Wherever they sit now (I hope it is with my parents on the most beautiful cloud in heaven), I send them love. They saved a soul, mine.

Another two angels appeared in my junior year. My new roommate, Alma, was beautiful, bright, and kind. We both married Sigma Nu brothers from Butler University and remained friends throughout her life, via her visits from California, and thanks to the telephone.

And Sister Mary Jane Peine, the Dean of Drama and Art…she was something special. She spoke what she thought, she lectured me when it was needed, and she taught me more than any professor *ever* did.

She also saved me. At the end of my sophomore year, I had serious fatigue and depression secretly listed in my diary. Sister Mary Jane must have realized that and she took care of it. She marched herself to the "office" and told them that I had had enough kitchen duty, that she needed somebody to clean the art department, and that I could do that. Cleaning the art department was a job twice a week, instead of a job three times a day for seven days. I was so relieved. Not only did I have more time to study, but she worked with me on my English, put me in plays, and became my friend. All she asked for all this was decent behavior.

Sister Mary Jane and I kept in touch throughout life. Years later, I kept telling her how talented my daughters were in the theater, which she loved. When Marika played the part of Anita in *West Side Story*, my husband and I took Sister out to dinner and to Cathedral High school's theatre to see Marika's work…

And Sister agreed with me, that my daughter was much better on the boards than her mother. In her outspoken way, Sister said:

"I wish I could have had HER in my classes!"

Oh, how I loved her.....

## another super angel

**MARILYN, WHO HAD JUST** graduated from Northwestern University in 1949, was enjoying her grand European tour when she received a request from friends of her parents.

They were involved with refugee students and wondered if Marilyn would be interested in spending time with some refugee students who were recipient of scholarships in America.

Being adventuresome, Marilyn packed her rucksack, and traveled to the castle *Hohenaschau*, where eight of us lucky students were spending a week prior to departing from Europe, learning about our colleges, America, and a few basic words in English.

She was perfect for this job. She was bright, fun, and serious when needed, and she spoke German. We learned a lot from Marilyn, and loved her, and promised to be in touch with her in America.

Some of us did, others not.

I did. As soon as I unpacked my suitcases, on December 2, 1949, I called Marilyn. "I am in the USA," I began.

"Could you spend Christmas with me and my family in Skokie, Illinois?" she answered.

There were not too many Cadillacs waiting for people at the Grayhound bus station in Chicago Illinois, USA. But there was one. Sitting in it were Marilyn and her father. They were waiting for ME…

Miracle of miracles…and a joyous, joyous, beautiful Christmas!

Beautiful Chicago, beautiful Christmas trees in beautiful stores. I particularly fell in love with one, Saks Fifth Avenue. And Mrs. Loeppert selected the most beautiful pair of pajamas I had ever seen, as a gift for me. I LOVED those pajamas. Years later, when the pajamas worn to shreds, my husband suggested, gently, that I get rid of them.

Marilyn visited me often in Indianapolis. I loved her family, and some years later her dear, young niece, Sue, moved to Indianapolis, and became our friend.

After I graduated from Marian College, I was hoping to continue my studies in Chicago. By then, Marilyn was married and living in California. Her parents invited me to stay with them until I found a place to live. I spent a few delightful weeks with them, until I moved into a dorm at Northwestern University, began taking some classes in their downtown branch, and found a job.

I loved Chicago, loved the Loepperts, and loved Marilyn....

Who, after her two sons were born, had a baby daughter, whom she named Márta.

AND she was a bridesmaid in my wedding.

I will never forget the day she called me in recent years and we spent an hour on the phone, a week before she headed toward heaven, still smiling about our lives, our adventures, and our long, wonderful friendship.

A refugee and her friend, who drove a Cadillac.

# and there was a rainbow

**MARIAN** was a woman's college in my day. We did not see boys or men too often on campus. I was still hurting a little about the man I lost when I left him for America.

My roommate in my junior year, Alma, decided that I needed to meet "boys," and stop living in the past. She was dating a tall, red-headed Sigma Nu from Butler University, and the "brothers" all liked her. So, for some dance, she fixed up several Marian girls with Butler Sigma Nu boys.

My date's name was Michael (I always fell for that name). He had dark hair and was from New Jersey. We got along quite well.

For a while I was teased by the song, "When it's apple blossom time, in Orange, New Jersey, we'll make a peach of a pair." But Michael was a decent, nice guy, and he had a girlfriend in said Orange… and he told me, and we stayed friends.

Sitting on my left side, however, sat a tall, handsome Sigma Nu named Bill. I don't remember who he was fixed up with. He was not interested in me, but he was very interested in my "foreignness" and my having lived through World War II.

Some days after the dance, Alma informed me that "that" Bill (last name Blades) was driving around Marian's campus, in his Studebaker convertible, and she knew for sure that he was going to ask me out.

I was not particularly interested. Plus, a Butler girl I'd met at my job at Wasson's Department store knew Bill and his family and said, "Just do not run into his parents."

"Why?"

"They will not like that you are Catholic, and a foreigner."

leaves from an unexpected life 67

Amen.

But my roommate, Alma, kept talking about this Bill, and how great he was, and what fun it would be if I dated him. We could double date. And we did. One evening I went with Alma and Russ, and Bill, to his house, to watch their new BIG television. His parents were out...

But not for long. They got home, and they were delightful, kind, friendly, welcoming, certainly not as I'd heard them described. Still, I was scared....

When we got ready to go back to Marian for our 11:00 p.m. curfew, Mr. Blades (the father) wondered why Butler girls had to be back on campus so early. And he looked at me, and I had to tell him that I was not a Butler girl, but a Catholic Marian girl, and hearing me stutter, he had to know, that I was a "foreigner."

But Wilma and KB Blades were not like that, nor was Bill's sister, Betty, and her husband, Tom. They were the most wonderful in laws I could ask for.

Because I married Bill Blades.

We spent two wonderful years in Germany, after he was drafted, and Mommikins (my mother-in-law) spent a wonderful summer with us.

Then Bill went back to his job at the Indianapolis Star. I worked at a joy job at L. S. Ayres, we had three children, bought a house in the Meridian Kessler area, had dogs, cats, and even strange pets. I remember ant farms....

And our children had the most wonderful grandparents. Wilma Donner Blades had been the prettiest girl in Hope, Indiana, and in time became the prettiest grandmother. She played the piano, the organ and the violin. She had a silver laughter and a golden heart. KB (Kenneth

Bill and I in the *Indianapolis Star*

Marshall Blades) was also from Hope, Indiana. They were high school sweethearts, and married as soon as he graduated from Indiana University. He was well read, smart, and handy around the house. I still cherish and use tables we designed, and he built for me. Being surrounded by women (Bill's sister, Betty, and her husband, Tom, had two beautiful daughters, Stephanie and Melissa), he was delighted when our son, Michael, was born. He was a very special man.

And everything was pretty wonderful in our world.

Until it was not.

Then we got a divorce.

After the bitterness softened, we became friends again. We often had dinners together. He visited Marika and her husband, Brian, in several homes where Brian's job took them. He loved Key West, where Michael and Kathy lived. He was at each of our children's weddings. And we all attended a cookout at Michele and Jerome's house on Father's Day in 2005.

Two weeks after, Bill died of lung cancer. Michele and I held his hands, and told him that we loved him.

After his funeral services, on a gray, gray day, we all stood in front of the restaurant, and out of nowhere there was the most beautiful rainbow in the sky.

I think it was Michael who said, "That's Dad."

I have a lot of crystal and sunshine in my condo. They usually create little rainbows, when they meet a sunbeam.

But even on gray, dark days, if I am sad or troubled, a tiny rainbow dances around, with glorious color, around me and the furniture in my snow white condo. I have no idea where they come from in the darkness.

But somehow I feel it is Bill Blades and he is around, with his smile and his laughter, to cheer me up. Maybe this is a sign of my growing years, but whatever it is, it does cheer me up.

It is SO Bill…

I wish he could have known his grandsons as grown-ups. They love books, as much as he did. They dress with the same effortless style as he did.

And they are gentlemen, as he was…

*Grandsons:* You love books as much as he did, and you dress with his same effortless style. He would have been so proud of you!

## waiting for the year 1972

**IT'S NEW YEAR'S DAY 1972.** That's logical, since last night was New Year's Eve 1971. My husband, Bill B. and I, our hearts touched by love, joy and all that holiday spirit, which all too briefly float through the air during this season, had made a major decision. We would spend New Year's Eve at home, and we would let the children stay up until midnight. This would serve a double purpose: we would spend this special evening within the warmth of our family, and we would avoid all that traffic, and all those crazy people on the roads. At least, that's what I called them. Our eleven-year-old daughter, Marika, immediately corrected me.

"You mean, all those drunks," she said.

We did. We spent New Year's Eve at home. And it was fun. It was. However, at the fresh new dawn of 1972, I had serious second thoughts. As I descended the stairs, still worn out from all that family warmth and tranquility the night before, I found only Marcel Marceau, the dog, sitting majestically on the couch, in the living room.

He was exhausted, too. He gave me a dirty look. It said loud and clear:

"How could you possibly let me fall asleep down here, in this mess, last night?" He was right. How could I?

The living room was blanketed by tiny paper strips. There were five pairs of kicked-off shoes, in assorted sizes, empty soda and root beer cans, the crumbly remnants of chips in myriad bowls, one sleeping bag, and scattered pillows, meant to be scattered elsewhere, all over the floor. It looked as if there had been twenty-five of those crazy people at our party—I mean, drunks.

It had been quite an evening. The children, aforementioned Marika, her "much older" sister, twelve-year old Michele, and brother Michael, draped themselves all over the furniture. That, after somewhat heated discussions about who "gets" each end of the couch. Mature beyond his years, seven-year-old Mike solved the problem by appearing with his Snoopy sleeping bag. The girls each had a couch corner. With eyelids half-mast by 10:30, they were waiting for Guy Lombardo to come on TV at 11:30. Father, in turn, was waiting for a football game to come on, on the same TV, also at 11:30.

In the meantime, they consumed everything edible in the house. Then, they all fell asleep. At midnight, Bill interrupted his focused watching of the game, and we merrily popped open dozens of little paper bottles, which spit out, amidst great noise, wonderful assorted colored confetti strips. These happy New Year sounds awakened the children and our most dignified dog. It took me forty-five minutes, and a long midnight walk, to calm down the dog, and an hour and half to get the children to bed, still wondering what happened to Guy Lombardo.

And so we rang in New Year's Day 1972, a time to reflect upon the wonders of the past year.

Each year, I liked to gather my family to my bosom and reflect together, after they helped me clean up the aftermath and haul the garbage bags out of the living room. Since there were four Bowl games on the magic machine, Bill B, for one, was out. He did not want to reflect. He wanted to watch football. Also, he was never too fond of garbage bags.

Since my entire knowledge of football was and still is limited to two facts, I hardly made the best viewing companion. In spite of this, I still find these two facts fascinating. Football star Broadway Joe Namath is of Hungarian descent, and he has, according to *Ladies' Home Journal*, a white fur rug in his living room. These facts are a great deal more interesting to me than say, "touchdowns," whatever they are. Having been born and raised in Hungary, I know that his name should be spelled with two e's, instead of two a's, Nemeth instead of Namath, and the name would mean "German" in Hungarian.

And the idea of that fur on his floor always fascinated me! The closest we came to white fuzz in our living room was the stuffing coming out of the arm of the couch. It was always artfully covered up with orange and avocado pillows. Except, when we had company. Then Bill sat there, messing up the pillows, to prove to the world that we too had fuzzy white stuff in our living room. Unfortunately it was in the form of a torn-up couch arm, not in the form of sophisticated floor covering.

On the first day of a brand new year, I wanted like to reflect. But where? Obviously, the living room, which housed the TV, was out. So was the master bedroom. There Marika was stretched out on the majestic brass bed, talking on the phone to her best friend, Eleanor. She had not talked to Eleanor since midnight last night; they had an enormous amount of catching up to do. She stopped chatting occasionally, to quite audibly admonish her little brother, Michael. He was in his room playing with his best friend, neighbor Sarah, who is six. Each time Marika interrupted her conversation with

Eleanor, and erupted, meant that Michael had snitched her brand new tape-recorder and was playing roving reporter with Sarah.

Michele's room was totally out. We had given her a darling plaque for Christmas. In vibrant colors, it read "Wanted: A Clean Room." She did not find it darling at all. But then again, Michele was a teenager, after all, who had just read an article in some insipid magazine, by some smart-aleck psychiatrist, stating that geniuses had better things to do than cleaning their rooms. She had declared herself a genius, and adopted the author of this article as her all-knowing guru. I wanted to hang him with his broom. Or else, have him come to clean Michele's room.

Of course, there was the dining room. Unfortunately, the dining table had been elected to display Michael's major Christmas present, the electric train. Bill was positively out of his mind with excitement about this train, ever since he spent a fortune on it. Michael did not pay any attention to it at all. He liked both Marika's tape recorder and the plastic gadget that threw out little plastic discs, gun fashion. He had bought it, unbeknownst to me, with his savings, at Hamaker's drugstore.

It terrified the dog, and his sisters. All for $1.95.

The dining room's serving table was also occupied by genius Michele. There she sat, since the dining room table was taken by the electric train. She was using the "good" typewriter to write a play, to be called "Jane Eyre." She was to write it, produce it, direct it, and star in it. But she did not want to write it in her own room, because who could find an inch of uncovered surface?

That left me the kitchen. Now I loved the kitchen. I mean I loved to look at it. I had just redecorated it. Everything was bright and new. Except the stove, which we'd inhherited from Bill's parents. Unfortunately, it worked beautifully. It also dated back to the year when Bill was born.

Since there was no suitable typewriter space in my bright orange and yellow kitchen, I could not reflect there. The kitchen also reminded me of cooking-related chores, not my favorite. So I reflected in the dinette, with the "bad" typewriter, which I bought for Michele at the Junior League Next to New Shop. The ribbon was somewhat askance, and the "G" was sticking. I tried to reflect without "great, good, and gracious" or any other g-words. Michele, however, was (g)racious enough to keep popping in to fix the ribbon and jiggle the "G." Marika was (g)ood, still talking to Eleanor. Michael and Sarah were (g)reat, only interrupting me when they needed Coke and cookies.

Bill also popped in—during the commercials.

"What on earth are you doing?" he asked.

"I am reflecting. I am starting my memoirs," I said.

"Why don't you use the 'good' typewriter?" he asked and, without waiting for an answer, disappeared.

The game was on again.

Happy New Year!

# joy at the emporium

**I MET JUDIE AT PS #70,** which was actually the reason we chose the area where we bought our house. PS #70 was hailed as one of the best schools in Indianapolis. Michele and Marika loved it, as did Judie's two children, Wendy and Willie. We were on the committee for a talent show at the school, recruited as "creative" mothers.

The talent show was a huge success. As was our meeting. Judie and I had a number of shared interests. We also found out that we were both married to men named Bill, and the two Bills knew each other from Shortridge High School.

And, just as I was so excited to have found a soulmate whose kids liked the "theatre" as did mine, Judie informed me of her wonderful news. They were packing up their Volkswagen bus, their kids and their Siamese cat, and they were off for a year of touring Europe.

So I went back to my being wife, mother, *hausfrau* and clubwoman, which was not all that bad…but since my youngest, Michael, was almost ready for pre-K, the itch for "something else" appeared more frequently.

The YEAR in Europe went by faster than I thought…and on one day my phone unexpectedly rang. It was Judie, back home again in Indiana, ready to change my life dramatically.

"Helloooo, this is Judie calling," said a sweet voice and after a slight pause, "how would you like to buy a house with me?"

Judie was thirsting for new adventure. The business she started that manufactured monster-cycle molds had paled and now that she had passed her real-estate test and sold a few houses, she was ready for a new challenge.

How does a person answer a question like that? I reached for a cigarette (in those days), gulped three times, and said, "Well…"

After all, I was a college graduate.

However, I did not say, "No."

We did have a family conference. Bill Blades, being a man, wanted more details. I said that I wanted a summer project, and re-doing a little house in the neighborhood with Judie sounded like a perfect answer to my dreams!

So we hunted for pennies in cookie jars, old German beer mugs, and in the creases of all the upholstered furniture, as I reassured Bill B that I could not live without partaking in the renaissance of this little house. He finally gave in, and with a somewhat questionable smile agreed to finance my future.

I could not wait to meet Judie at the house. We sat on the floor of the porch and sealed our deal, with nary a handshake. Sitting on the wooden beam deck of this neglected little gem, we counted my half of the money for the down payment.

It was in cash.

That summer we rolled up our shirtsleeves, and worked, worked, worked…like devils. The shaded backyard was joyously taken over by our five children. To this day they consider it the best summer of their lives. The yard was full of wonderful surprises, like dead birds. They had magnificent funerals for the birds, wrote and played plays, looked like escapees from an orphanage, and in general loved their newly discovered world of neglected children.

The Bills appreciated our small steps of success. Before Judie and I touched the house, we cut the grass, trimmed the bushes, and planted geraniums.

"It already looks better," we said.

Indiana summers are not known to be pleasant. They are hot, humid, and generally unbearable. Our little house was truly christened with the sweat of our brow. We did everything... well, not everything. Bill N was taking classes in Baltimore and he supervised us on the weekends. I had no idea that, besides being a professor at Butler University, he also could build a house, all by himself. The Bills, however, were kind and praised our little accomplishments. I was terribly proud of painting stucco.

I had never done it before.

The house began to shape up. The icky aqua paint coat was replaced by a soft green, black shutters were hung, and once the outside was done, we attacked the inside: two little bedrooms, an adorable small bathroom, an all-white kitchen, and a happy, sun-filled living room. Everything was scrubbed to shiny clean, repainted—all done, except the living room ceiling. It was pretty bad, as were our finances, and fancy acoustic tile was not in our plans. So then what? We found a lovely red, white and blue patterned fabric for the curtains, which I sewed joyfully, but the ceiling. What would cover up the horrid condition best? Best? Of course, navy blue BURLAP!

Has anybody ever covered a ceiling with LONG strips of very, very heavy glue-covered burlap standing on twin ladders?

I know two people, who swore *never, ever again...*

Our friends stopped by periodically to see our progress. They all said that they'd always wanted to do something like this. Really? Because we never saw a beauty-shop all summer, and our wardrobe consisted of grimy Bermuda shorts and glue covered t-shirts, while our friends came by beautifully coifed, tanned, en route to the club, to the pool, to the tennis courts, and to Europe.

As we stood on top of ladders, we perspired profusely. We sawed, painted, scrubbed, disciplined our children, and laughed a lot, and on one early fall day we decided that is was done. And it was wonderful, and we had done most of it.

There was only one more problem. What to do with the little house? Surely, after such a love-affair with it, we could not possibly sell it!

Somewhere along the way, the idea of a shop was conceived, and I am sure that it was born in the wee hours of a morning, when Judie did her best thinking.

And out of such a wonderful summer, the idea of The EMPORIUM was born. And what followed was one of the happiest seven-year stretches of my life. It would all unfold right down the street from the site of our summer project.

Even after all these years, just thinking of it makes me smile. I think of a most special, wondrous, beautiful friend, named Judie and her amazing husband, Bill, and their just-as-interesting children…

And their fascinating granddaughter, who is a librarian, and who is my friend on FACEBOOK!

## she was not a bunny rabbit

**NYUSZI** in America.

My wonderful, beautiful mother, Nyuszi.

As I child, I called my parents Mama and Papa. They liked that. I did NOT. My friends called their parents in a more modern way, Anyuka and Apuka.

Of course, I wanted that, too.

Father did not go for the modernization. My mother did not mind, so we went half way, and I called my mother "Anyuszika."

That ended up being Nyuszi, which in Hungarian means bunny rabbit.

She was Hungarian all right, but not even close to a bunny. She was porcelain beautiful, and Hercules strong.

Thanks to the lovely American officer in Grohn who sped up her voyage to America, she followed me in just a month.

For DPs (displaced persons), as we were, we needed a job and a home, certified on paper.

Those who had no contact in America, the NCWC or other welfare organizations helped.

They found Nyuszi a job as a nanny in a home in Harrisburg, Pennsylvania.

Nyuszi did not know a lot about being a nanny. She just knew how to hire them, as she had hired Fraulein Lotte for me, long ago. Both she, and the nice young couple who sponsored her, realized that pretty soon. Their goodbyes were most friendly.

Aunt Pálma to the rescue! She was in Pennsylvania, too, in Oil City. She was a cook, and Uncle Ali was a chauffeur for a wealthy couple.

*My mother, Nyuszi*

Aunt Pálma, a cook...chef maybe, but NOT a cook. She informed Nyuszi and me that her boss, the "lady," was in Hungarian "mülady," a fake-lady whose taste was not the best. Aunt Pálma did not like the lady's taste in art.

Aunt Pálma and Uncle Ali welcomed Nyuszi with joy, but they did not stay in Oil City long. They soon moved to California, and Pálma ended up as head librarian at a college there.

Nyuzi, however, did stay in Oil City, Pennsylvania.

And she loved it…and Oil City loved her back.

As soon as possible, she moved into a sweet little cottage on Hasson Heights, bought a used sewing-machine, and she was in business. She was forty-nine years old, and learning English. She already knew Hungarian, French and German, and she knew how to sew.

She was amazing.

Pretty soon she knew everybody in Oil City. Aunt Pálma's "mülady" became first her client, then her friend.

As her business grew, she moved to a larger house downtown, which was on the way home from the country club for many of her friends, who stopped by to "visit with Martha." Her coffee pot was constantly plugged in!

She became the queen of weddings, creating for the brides, to the mothers-in-law, exquisite gowns, delivered always with a smile.

She became an active member on the board of her church, the Trinity United Methodist Church, and in everything involving classical music.

She was member of the Tuesday Musical, and president of Shubert Musical and Literary Club, and the Zonta Club.

I spent wonderful summers and Christmases with her. I had a job at the department store and met very interesting friends, who went to colleges I had never heard of…Bennington, Smith, and Vassar.

The first time I took Bill Blades to Oil City was at Christmas. Opening the front door, he gazed at the Christmas tree, lit up with burning candles, somewhat surprised.

He loved Nyuszi, and she him.

And so did his parents, Wilma and KB. When Nyuszi became ill, they helped me in moving her to Indianapolis, to live with them in their third floor apartment. She loved it there too and loved her grandchildren. Michele embroiders like she did. And I am so happy that Marika got to know her, and Michael a little too.

She was some Grandmere! I never saw her in jeans or pants or flat shoes. It was always high heels in Nyuszi's world.

In any situation, she remained as noble as she was born. She left us on New Year's Eve, 1971. I played the CD of her favorite opera, *János Vitéz* (John the Hero). It remains a difficult evening for me.

*Édesanyám*...my mother.

## return to hungary

*"**NEM KELL** nékem a világon semmi, csak mégegyszer tudnék hazamenni...."*

A Balázs and Berényi Hungarian song, translated, perhaps poorly:

"I would not ask for anything in the world, if I could only go home ONCE more......"

It played in my mind often, as time went by. *Just once, oh, please, just once...*but I made a promise to my mother that I would not go back to Hungary while the Soviets ruled there. That was in the year 1972. Amazingly fast it was 1991, and in 1991 the last Soviet troops left Hungary.

And I was beginning the think of the possibilities of a trip.

To *Magyarország* (Hungary), my cradle....

Just ONCE!

And as the years went by, I thought of it more, and more. I mentioned this to my kids. They, all three of them, wanted to join me. However, Michele was raising four boys and could not leave, and Michael could not leave his job. Bummer...but Marika and her husband Brian thought that would be doable.

Of course I mentioned this to my friends. Lolly thought that would be a great trip with her two children, since their father had Hungarian background. She mentioned this to her brother, Fritz, also my dear friend. They all wanted to join in this adventure, as they felt that my heart needed some help in this huge undertaking.... and they were right.

I was more than excited!

And the work began. Passports brought up to date. What-to-do-in-Budapest books bought. Dates studied. And of course the questions: "What do we wear to a part of the world that is not yet used to a lot of tourists?" and "Where else other than Budapest should we go?"

My beloved Szentes was important to me. As was Kecskemét, where I was born, and where I hoped to find my long-forgotten birth certificate.

Lolly chose to stay in Budapest. Her kids, Anne and Tom, spent some time with us before they took off to find some adventure and youth hostels.

Fritz wanted to see *everything*....

Brian was interested in visiting Herend, to explore a possible porcelain line for Saks Fifth Avenue and a crystal fabric.

And Marika had a most interesting idea: "We will be so close, why not Transylvania, now Romania?" (Both my parents' birthplaces.) *Brilliant.*

She had no idea what a difficult job she'd volunteered for. But she did it! She had trains, cities and villages, hotels and guides all lined up in a row.

And, on a sunny May day, ready or not, we each went to our airports, and with a smile and a prayer, began our Hungarian adventure.

I arrived first. There was no time to kiss the ground, as I'd dreamed I would upon arrival. But all around me there was a strange, magical happening: everyone spoke Hungarian!

Even my taxi driver spoke Hungarian! The drive to our hotel, in Budapest's heart, a well known old friend, the Astoria, was gray. Everything seemed gray. There were very few cars on the roads, and people were carrying what I thought were grocery bags, which were gray. Certainly Budapest did not seem as happy and colorful as I remembered.

Then I realized that it was not too long ago that the Soviets had been there, and my beloved country needed time to heal.

The Astoria was there, just as I remembered, with still a lovely foyer, and a smiling gentleman behind a desk. He welcomed me in a soft, Hungarian-spiced English. I answered him in my native language, and his smile was even sweeter as he greeted me, with Hungary's old, beautiful greeting:

*"Isten hozta..."* (The Lord brought you...)

...and He did.

# budapest

**PRETTY SOON** the lovely Biedermeier foyer of the Astoria was filled with Americans, speaking English, tired, but excited. All were there, except Marika and Brian, who were coming from Vienna on a hydrofoil on the Danube.

After lunch by the Danube, I walked over to the hydrofoil station, and soon they were on Hungarian soil. It was one of the happiest moments of my life.

My children in my birth country. I missed Michele and Michael, and there on the Danube shore, I said a silent prayer, that one day, one wonderful future day, they too will be arriving in Hungary.

We did have a great time. Budapest, divided as Buda and Pest by nine bridges, began to be more joyous. The once elegant Váci *utca* (street) was filled with Hungarian pottery and embroidery. The glorious Andrássy *ut* (boulevard) is terminated by the *Hösök Tere* (Heroes Square), Hungary's Millenial Monument, where one finds the sculpture of *Arpád* (my ancestor) the *Kende* (king)

*Visiting my ancestor, Arpád*

on his horse, with his chieftains, who in the year 896 led his people to become Hungarians. The Opera, with the most gilded, glorious interior, is also on Andrássy *ut*.

Close by is the city park, which is next to the Erzsébet Noiskola (Elisabeth Women's School) where I went to boarding school, long ago. We received a lovely grand tour by the English teacher. The highlight of the tour was seeing the room dedicated to

*Erzsébet nöiskola in Budapest*

*The famous "red apron" uniform of the school*

the "Erzsébet Noiskola" with old pictures and a doll dressed in our famous red-aproned uniforms.

We walked through the city park, visiting some museums, and tracing the Danube shore by the Parliament. It is one of the world's most beautiful buildings, facing the Danube, and the oldest of the bridges, the chain bridge.

We heard some Hungarian gipsy music, filling my eyes with tears, at the Karpathia Restaurant. We ate lunch at the glorious New York Cafe, and enjoyed Dobos *torta* (cake) at the famous Gerbeaud Cafe.

We loved Buda, with the castle, on Castle Hill, and the ancient *Halászbástya* (Fisherman's Bastion). We saw the Gellért Mountain and the Gellért baths.

We covered Budapest, smiling, and laughing, and crying, and loving it.

# kecskemét

**LOLLY, ANNE, AND TOM** were ready to travel home. We knew that we would miss them, along with their curiosity and their joy. I was so happy to have shared Budapest with them. It was a sad goodbye as we—Marika, Brian, Fritz and I—were getting ready for the Hungary's *Alfold* (great plain), Kecskemét.

We journeyed eastward from Budapest to the limitless lowland, the city where my father opened his engineer office, and where I was born.

Kecskemét is the capitol of the mostly agricultural area between the Tisza and the Danube rivers, with its most famous product, the fiery apricot brandy, and a beautiful, lavishly decorated Town Hall. It was where we were heading, in search of my birth certificate.

Although marks of late nineteenth and early twentieth century prosperity graced the downtown area, Hungary's businesses were still soft and sweet. In the center of the lovely Jozsef Katona Square (Katona was a famous Hungarian playwright) stood the beautiful art nouveau City Hall. We got there at lunch time, and lunch time was "closed" time. A nice lady, however, told us that during the lunch hour we could go and buy stamps, which are needed to obtain any birth certificate. Which meant that I had another hour suffering before I could find out if I was born, or not.

Yes, I was. The nice lady had found my birth certificate, and she printed it out. It was very pretty. And she found something more: the address of where I lived with my parents, after I was born. We lived on a street also named for Jozsef Katona, a lovely building of apartments, which we visited. A very old gentlemen thought that he remembered my parents (at least he thought so) and he showed us around.

If felt so wonderful to leave Kecskemét with such an important, properly printed and stamped piece of paper.

Then it was back to the rented car, with a nice hired driver, and off we were to another town in the great plain, the town I remembered best and still call my most beloved, Szentes.

## szentes

**THE MINUTE** we drove by the train station (where I spent a lot of time when I was in school in Budapest) I felt at home...finding a somewhat sad home. As we drove toward the city center, the Kossuth Square, I realized that Szentes must have been a scene of serious fighting in World War II. The beautiful City Hall, built in 1910, in neo baroque style, somewhat magically, still stood. Most buildings around it did not. Two other beautiful old buildings, the Petofi Hotel and the Toth Jozsef Theatre, were not as fortunate.

Around the corner from City Hall was the street I was looking for: Toth Jozsef Street, named for one of Hungary's famous actors.

We parked the car by a building very well known to me, my elementary school, which faced my church.

As now, like I did so many years ago, I faced Toth Jozsef utca.

The left side of the street was almost totally ruined. My heartbeat was dangerously beating by then. But we kept walking, and somehow behind the ruins I saw the tall green iron fence, and beyond the fence, happily, still standing, stood our house.

Number 28.

By now, all my Kleenex was used up.

But feeling rather brave, I did walk up to the gate and reached for the bell by the door, when appeared an adorable little boy.

"Are your parents here?" I asked.

And they were, and they were nice. Seeing my tears, they decided that I needed something to drink, and they invited us in.

To their house.

Imre Szibrik, the Mayor of Szentes lived there now, with his wife Rozsa, and their fourteen-year-old daughter and nine-year-old son.

They showed us the house, decorated very differently from ours. Ours was full of large paintings, wonderful antique Persian rugs, silver dishes with my mother's monogram (with the crown...) and many, many books. Seventy years later, the house still looked happy, full of sunshine, and nicely looking "now"... Nyuszi's huge garden, however, was in bad shape. The Szibriks had just bought the house, and the garden was their next job.

Not only were they so generous at their house, but they packed us in their car and gave us a grand tour of Szentes. Imre, very excited, told us about all the plans he had for Szentes. I saw his work in several upcoming visits to Szentes, and in a book about Szentes, in four languages, which was his idea, and which he gifted me on a later visit.

And I enjoyed their fourteen-year-old daughter so much, remembering myself at that age.

When I got home, I did some serious shopping, for things a fourteen year old would like, and sent them to another fourteen year old, who lived in a house in Toth Jozef Street 28.

From Imre, we learned a lot about what Szentes went through on that famous June day in 1933.

The last Soviet troops had left Hungary, just two years before our visit, in 1991.

The rebuilding of Szentes was on the way.

Imre drove us to a favorite spot of mine, a part of Szentes that was seemingly untouched by the war.

The city park.

And in the heart of the park we glimpsed "the strand," the swimming pool where I spent my summers, with my mother, and her friends, and my friends. Such lovely summers. We all had little buildings where we kept our towels and bathing suits. Almost every day we spent at the "strand."

And it still was all there: a restaurant and the large pool, which also was used as practice pool for the Hungarian water-polo team.

Next to the pool was a wonderful little city: thermal camping. It was such fun to have dinner by the pool, and spend the night in tiny huts! Enjoying the symphonies of the frogs, all around us. Very loud, happy frogs. Brian thought they were playing more Beethoven than Brahms.

Next morning we left Szentes, ready for the next adventure. But not before we met a gentleman who, in English, apologized to us for not having many restaurants rebuilt in Szentes. He said, "If you want to eat at a Burger King, you will have to go to Szeged." (Szeged is a larger city.)

How sweet, but we would not have changed our chicken paprika dinner in the city park for Burger King, for all the tea in China!

# herend

**HEREND,** the beautiful Hungarian porcelain, is actually made in Herend. Herend is west of Budapest, in the transdanubia part of the country. The facility is absolutely beautiful, as it is situated in sort of a garden setting.

We learned that most of the people who worked there also lived in the neighborhood.

Herend has a long and most interesting history. Through peace and wars, it remained a factory. In 1976, it celebrated is one-hundred-fiftieth anniversary. And to this day it remains Hungary's pride, delivering porcelain to over forty countries.

We just *had* to go to Herend, to see how they created this beautiful porcelain.

Brian had a couple of business interests in Hungary. Saks Fifth Avenue, whose lawyer he was, carried Herend wares. He also wanted to visit a home-furnishing company. His assistant worked on the plans, and off we went.

In our rented car, with our rented driver, again, through a somewhat soft, hilly part of Hungary, along the largest lake of the country, the Balaton, the two-hour trip from Budapest, was quite lovely.

We were gracefully greeted by the director of Herend, who gave us a most interesting personal tour of the factory. I always thought of Herend pieces as very pricey, but when we learned the many steps each piece goes through, I was amazed that they are not more costly.

Of all the steps we saw them go through, one of the last steps was the most amazing. Each piece is hand-painted by artists, each sitting in their little studio. *Amazing.*

I had a little personal interest in Herend, also. For my fourteenth birthday, my parents gifted me with Herend porcelain. I don't remember if it was for six or eight, but it was dinner ware, tea services, and all the dishes and accessories. My mother worked with the artist who was to paint them, and it was a personal design, just for me.

Of course, being fourteen years old, I was not that interested in porcelain dining sets. But my mother was very happy when the wooden boxes arrived. She opened a few, and we used some, just for JOY!

It was a very brief time of joy. When we fled from Hungary in 1944, my parents hid the boxes in the large air ducts in our apartment in Budapest, to be safe when we returned.

We never returned. The Herend china remained a memory, along with everything else we lost. But Herend stayed in our hearts.

*Michele's Herend porcelain pattern*

I was delighted when my daughter, Michele, chose beautiful, blue-designed Herend porcelain for her wedding china. And she uses it. On holidays on her beautifully set table, we all enjoy the beauty of Herend, and Michele's lovely taste.And I have a brilliant Santa, who leaves a Herend figure under the Christmas tree for me. It is my pride and joy, my Herend collection.

Joy!

So, when we were with the Director of Herend, I asked him if they possibly had any drawings, or any kind of paperwork of the china my mother ordered and purchased. He was so sorry, but he said all the records were destroyed, including the names Herend created for the order.

When our lovely visit came to an end, the director led us into the shop in the factory, and gifted each of us with a beautiful Herend china piece.

And he invited us to their beautiful dining room, where each table was set with different designed china, for lunch. Brian thanked him and explained that we had another appointment and could not stay, because his assistant had made an appointment with the home furnishing company and they were waiting for us for lunch.

We were delightfully greeted there, too, and led to an office, where chips and sodas were waiting for us.

It was not the end of the world, but Brian's assistant had mixed up the lunch, and the chips and sodas. We were supposed to have lunch at Herend, in their glorious dining room….

But it was still a great day!

## transylvania

**I WAS SO EXCITED** to even think of Transylvania—my mother's beloved Erdély—where she was born, where she married my father, and where she was so happy, loving her world and her mountains.

My son-in-law Brian was excited too. His grandfather was from Transylvania, until he was seven years old, when he immigrated to the USA. My daughter, Marika, was thrilled as well; she had planned the whole trip and it was not an easy job. Our friend, Fritz, who was traveling with us, was just as eager to make the journey.

So, four excited people arrived to Budapest's *Keleti Pályaudvar* (Budapest's Eastern Railway Terminal) with tickets in their pockets to Cluj Napoca (Kolozsvár), Romania. The express train was leaving the terminal at 7:40 a.m., arriving in Cluj at 16:08 (in our world, 4:08 p.m.).

The terminal alone was a happening. Built in 1891, in eclectic style, it was adorned with statues on the outside and beautiful frescoes inside.

The train was there, waiting just for us. It was very comfortable, with a nice dining car.

And off we went. I loved seeing every tree, every house, every hill we traveled by. This was Nyuszi's land (Nyuszi being my mother). We were simply sitting quietly, until two smiling, young soldiers came on the train to check our passports.

We were in Transylvania and the tears appeared. Eight hours seemed to go by faster than expected.

When we arrived in Cluj (Kolozsvár), a young man was holding a sign for us. He was waiting for us. His name was Yener, he spoke English, he knew where everything was, and he became a heaven-sent wonderful friend.

And he drove us to our hotel.

And he informed us that we had tickets to the opera that evening. What a beginning!

En route to the hotel, we drove by the statue of the Hungarian King, the beloved Máyás Király (King

Mathias), who was born in Kolozsvár in 1458. Known as "The Just," he ruled with interest in art and science, and had the largest royal library in the world. He was a well-loved King.

Brian's favorite old Hungarian quote was "King Mathias died, truth has gone."

The opera was beautiful—it was old and decked out in royal red velvet chairs. I could imagine my elegant grandfather (whom I did not know) there with my mother, who learned her love for classical music in this opera house. Oh my! And we were actually there.

The Köváry name, my mother's name, popped up in Kolozsvár quite a bit. There was and still is a street named for my great uncle, Laszlo Köváry, a well-known author of mostly Transylvanian history, and his brother, Endre Köváry, an artist, who was known as having painted over fifty paintings of Emperor/King Franz Joseph.

We saw the museum, the house where King Mátyás was born, and the Köváry street. We walked on well-used, old streets, and we ate original stuffed cabbage and other long-forgotten special dishes of Erdély. It was wonderful.

But Yener had more surprises for us.

He showed us a book by Laszlo Köváry about castles in Transylvania, drawing our attention to the chapter about a Kendeffy fort (Kendeffy was my maternal grandmother's family name). It was a fort built on top of a mountain in the seventh century, now in ruins. Köváry wrote of this fort in the southern part of Transylvania, where tourists seldom go. It is mostly visited by hunters, chamois hunters. And that is where we hoped to go, to see that fort. Yener looked us over and said, "You do not look like chamois hunters."

*Marika and Brian at the Kendeffy Castle*

He continued, "I had a terrific time finding a hotel in that area. When I finally did find one, I didn't know what to expect—it is the Malomvizi Kendeffy castle."

We could hardly believe him.

The next day he drove us there…and there it was, my grandmother's family ancestral castle. Now a hotel.

It was built in 1782 by Count Alexis Kendeffy of Malomviz, and his wife, Countess Christina Bethlen.

Amazing.

The hotel staff was delightful. When they found out that Marika and I were, somewhere in the past, related to the "family," they became even more helpful.

They showed us the inside of the church and letters from other Kenndeffy relatives. They then told us to go to the ancient chapel, where scratched deep on a rock wall, you can still read:

*"Tobias Décsi, de Boronya, Hic fuit pedagogus (teacher) to Nicolai Kendeffi, 1692"*

Also amazing!

Next we found the ruins of the fort. The fort is described in a Laszlo Köváry book as:

"We don't speak of fairies and giants at this fort, just about knights, and ladies. One story is about the lady, Ilona Kendeffi, who loved to sit on the balcony of the fort, waiting for her husband to come home from the wars, spinning silk ribbons, and letting them fall into the dark depth, around the fort."

We began to climb the mountain road leading up to the fort the mountaintop. I knew that I could not possibly go further up. Brian, Fritz, and I tried to talk Marika out of climbing the mountain, but she was determined to go up to see the ruins. Yener wanted to go with her. And as if from the air, four young Romanian girls appeared. Knowing the way up, they offered to guide them.

Brian and I had a very difficult couple of hours at the base, scared of the mountain, scared of the girls we did not know. Just scared.

But Marika did it, and she brought us mementos.

I still have and cherish the rocks she found. And secretly, I was very, very proud of her!

Back at the castle, they were thinking of dinner for us and asked us what we would like. We had had somewhat enough of tourists menus, and wondered if they could make us chicken soup. We waited for a while, and the chicken soup appeared…absolutely delicious chicken soup from their home-grown chickens, behind the castle.

We were sad to leave this beautiful part of Transylvania, and our lovely new friends from the castle. As we were saying goodbyes, the lady at the desk, with whom we could not chit-chat since we did not speak Romanian, smiled at us and handed both Marika and me each an exquisite hand-woven purse.

Our tears were our thank yous.

Yener had another surprise for us.

When we were in Budapest, around Vaci Street, where Transylvanian women were selling their beautiful hand-embroidered goods. We made friends with one of the ladies who spoke Hungarian. When I told her that we were going to Transylvania, she invited us to her home there, mentioning that she has invited a number of people, and nobody ever visited.

Yener was going to fix this.

He found the house, with some difficulty, driving on rough streets, not used to automobiles.

Our friend, Jutka from the Vaci *utca*, could not

*Treasure room in Transylvania with Fritz*

believe her eyes. And she showed us her rooms, filled with the most beautiful embroidered everything. She called them their "treasure rooms," and that is what they were.

Next stop was Vajdahunyad (Hunadora), next to the most famous castle of the Hunyady family (a copy of it is in Budapest, at the city park). It is also the Vajdahunyad of rich mines, where my father was a leading mining engineer. As we walked around it seemed a rather sad town. The mines were long closed, and we could not find any relatives in the cemetery.

Temesgyarmat (Giarmata), where my father was born, was a different story. It is a sweet, dear village, with church bells ringing and a cemetery full of Kilczers. My father had had seven brothers and sisters, and a lot of uncles and aunts, none I ever met before now. They greeted me now, from beautiful sculptured graves, as if I was a relative... and I was, a relative.

Since we were so close to Temesvár (Timisoara) from Temes Gyarmata, we decided to drive over there. Temesvár meant my father to me. The seventh son in his family, he became the first to graduate from college, after high school (*gimnazium*) in Temesvár.

Temesvár was the largest city in the Bánát, and had the third highest population of Romanian cities. Known for art and culture, it was often called "small Vienna."

My father loved it.

Romania suffered for twenty years under the strong Communist hands of Nicolae Ceausescu until 1989, when on Temesvár's Liberty Square, the Romanian Revolution began and spread through the country.

And the torturer who owned the world's second largest palace, and hardly fed the people, was killed by execution by firing squad.

Temesvár bloomed, and we loved it.

We also loved our wonderful walks in the park, great theater, beautiful restaurants, and even a department store, a very fine one at that.

Our friend Fritz absolutely fell in love with a wood-burning stove. We thought it would be a bit complicated, however, to ship the stove from Timisoare to Dixon, New Mexico, USA, where he lived.

It was a sad morning when we closed our suitcases and prepared to leave not just Temesvár, but the Bánát and Transylvania.

It was especially difficult to leave Yener, who made our travels even more magical.

Because it was just that…

Magical!

# thirty-five glorious gallery years

**JUDIE AND I BOUGHT** a little house on the corner of 49th and Penn Street in Indianapolis. As we fixed it up, our secret hope became to open a little shop there.

Initially we could not get the zoning permit to have a business in a residential area. It just happened that there was a business area just down the street, with a huge RENT sign on its door. It was a business building with a Frame

Designs frame shop on one side, and a hair salon on the other, framing the empty center.

It was not empty for long. In a matter of days, with our lovely red sign, EMPORIUM, hanging outside, the happiest gift shop in town was open.

Our neighbor shops were fine. Fred's hair salon was beautiful. Unfortunately we never had the time to visit it. On the other side, the framing establishment's work space was next to our storage space. It was owned by two young men, John and Ron, who had just graduated from Indiana University. Both were married to darling wives, and both had three children. We liked them and their families a lot.

They were hard workers, especially before Christmas. It seemed like everybody in Indianapolis wanted their gems framed for Christmas gifts.

The boys worked enormous hours. Judie and I learned some brand new words from next door. It was under-pressure swearing…we understood, and giggled. After seven years of fun and joy, we sold the Emporium.

From there, my first job was to hire somebody to clear the basement in our home. Other than having thrown anything that was in my way down into it, it was seldom visited. In the midst of enjoying this amazing happening, the phone rang, and it was John Mallon from Frame Designs. "Why don't you come over tomorrow? I have an idea," he said.

That was Monday. I went over on Tuesday, and by Wednesday I had a new job, running the Frame Designs shop, because they were building several Do It Yourself frame shops. They promised me two weeks of learning, but they'd forgotten that they were going fishing for two weeks. I began alone.

My first client who walked through the door, on my first framing day, brought in a rather difficult and interesting job. Fifteen photographs from a nude bathing camp, all put in one frame. He came in to pick it up on my day off. I often wondered if he liked the finished product.

To this day, nobody—not even John's wife, the business-minded and bright Barbara—remembers my start date as a frame designer.

But we do know that I stayed in their business for about thrity-five years, retiring in July 2006.

I learned to design frames, even measuring (I did, Barb) and writing up the tickets that we sent to the warehouse, where the work was done. I was even voted "Best Framer in Indianapolis," but I lost the unframed diploma, to be able to show it off.

I don't remember the dates, but I do remember that we moved quite a bit. John wanted to turn us into an art gallery with the framing. I loved that idea! He was way ahead of the city. We had a shop downtown, in the Barnes Thurnburg building, next to a beautifully restored old building on Massachusetts Avenue. The buildings were all white, one more beautiful than the other. But downtown was not ready for us yet. Still lovely memories.

John always had surprises. After a while, he and Ron went in different directions. But every year after that, there was a phone call from Ron, on Christmas eve, to wish me happy holidays. I was so touched that I forgave him for all the times he walked out of the store with my salary check still in his pocket.

John's *big* news was that he bought the oldest, most wonderful contemporary art gallery in Indianapolis, Editions Limited…lock, stock, and barrel, including the director and staff.

I turned every color on the color wheel from envy. There I was with a degree in art, and I was left a framer? I was not happy, but it did not last long. The director of Editions, who was actually very nice, was moving out of town.

I finally got the crown…my life's wish…being director of an art gallery.

We moved again, and again to better, and better spaces with Editions. The last, and final move was to Broadripple, where John and Barb bought a house for it. It was my dream job. We had about seventy artists in our stable and about four exhibits a year, and I had an office of my own—it was pure heaven. The Mallons' kids, Chris and Jack, grew and added fun to our staff. And what a staff! Amanda, Beth, Chris, Debbie, Jo, George, Kay, and Marietta.

We had shows for Peter Max, and then Garfield came to visit in person, with many framed portraits. We had solo shows with WilleFaust, Michael Leu, Carol Summers, Peter Kichell, Gary Bukovnik, Marcus Pierson, Fritz Kackley, Lolly Glasel, Paul Wandless, KP Sighn, Lois Templeton, and a few Márta Blades, too. I loved them all; I would need a book to list them all. So sorry….

YES, I DID love them all, a lot.

*The staff of Editions Limited welcomes Garfield to the gallery*

> *The end of an era,
> the beginning of a new journey.*
>
> Please join us Saturday April 23, 2005
> for an open house from 7 to 10 pm
> Editions Limited Gallery
> 838 E. 65th St., Indianapolis, IN 46220
>
> **To honor the career and celebrate the retirement of Marta Blades**
>
> Wine and Hors D'oeuvres
>
> Please RSVP
> 466-9940
> art@editionsltd.com

When I retired, the girls sent cards to all of our artists, with the request for a 4x4-inch painting for me. They ALL sent me this wonderful goodbye gift. John had them framed, and they were exhibited at my—oh my—absolutely elegant, well-attended, glorious retirement party.

Judie called it, "A tribute to all the joy you have brought to us all; all of us attuned in harmony..... what affection!"

The tribute goes to the Mallon family, the wonderful years, and all the wonderful people I worked with, or who just came to us for what we all loved so much—ART.

# finally settling down in the south

**THE LARGE, SQUARE** Andy Warhol 2006 calendar hung in the beloved old house, as it celebrated its one-hundred-fiftieth birthday.

Year after year, in the kitchen by the wall phone, for forty-five years, one art calendar replaced another, through the various, forever-changing renaissances of the house's décor. There were Michael Leu's smiling cats, Matisse's color-rich cut-outs, buildings wrapped in Hungary's national colors, red, white and green, Carol Summers' wondrous woodcuts, New York's sky scrapers, KOCO's brave, bold brushstrokes—all brightened the corner as the small squares of the calendar filled up with activities.

Year after year, Blue Birds and Brownie meetings, Sunday schools, baseball games, cheerleading practices, football games, play rehearsals, theater performances, ad club meetings, 500-mile race festivities, Junior League and Phoenix Theatre board meetings, Junior Symphony Ball plans, Herron Museum Saturday art classes, PTA, The Emporium boutique's staffing...days and hours filling our lives.

Bill and Márta, the parents, and Michele, Marika and Michael, the children, were the inhabitants of the house, where all of these activities filled the calendar pages. They and the pets—through the years, Schnitzel the dachshund, Noodles the cat, Pushkin the mutt, Marcel I the poodle, Frodo the Vizsla, Isobelt's seven black kittens (all named Munchkin, until we found homes for them), John Galt the adopted cat, Marcel II, and Savannah—beloved four legged members of the family. They were all in and out of the house, along with the humans.

One by one, through the years, the pets left for greener celestial pastures.

One by one, the family dispersed as well. The children chose colleges, became young adults following their bliss, and slowly and painfully the marriage dissolved, and there was only one person left at 5148 Park Avenue in Indianapolis, Indiana. One human, and one cat, sweet Savannah, and the ashes of the last happy dog, Marcel II.

So, in 2006 the last cat helped the last human with selling the house, packing up the house, and entrusting the favorite "stuff" to Mr. Stuart's fabulous moving company. The last cat and the last human then dried some tears, and with the oldest daughter Michele, travelled south, seeking warmer sunshine, bluer skies, a magical new world, and another daughter's loving arms.

My name is Márta, a.k.a. the last human of the house. This is the story of my journey from Kecskemét, Hungary, to Winston-Salem, in beautiful North Carolina, in the blessed United States of America, in the year of the Lord 2006.

## traded a kidney for a dog

**ON JULY 26, 2006,** with my daughter Michele at the wheel, and my sweet Savannah cat in her box on the back seat, I said good bye to my much loved, 150-year-old house, after living there for forty-five years.

"The time has come," the walrus said, "to speak of many things."

I got through my sixties, healthy as possible, nothing broken, nothing hurting, seemingly healthy as can be, until I reached my seventies.

Then, my arm began to bother me. That turned into a little more serious problem.

Breast cancer.

The doctors at the Indiana University hospital were wonderful, all three of my children were with me, and I was SO very fortunate. I did not need surgery.

There was a brand new wonder drug, Femara, that had just received FDA approval on January 10th, which happened to be my daughter Marika's birthday…it saved me.

Still, my children were worried. Yet Michele had four sons to take care of, and Michael lived pretty far away, plus he travelled a lot.

Marika and Brian volunteered. They said, "We will be so happy to take care of you. We cannot move to Indianapolis, but you could move to Winston-Salem."

And as soon as my old home was sold, and my new habitat in Winston-Salem was finished, I did, gratefully.

After two years of being built, with Brian and Marika's amazing oversight and help, the condo in

Winston-Salem, North Carolina's South side, downtown, was finished. The day of JOY arrived.

It was *beautiful!* All white—walls, ceilings, kitchen—just waiting for color in the paintings and oriental rugs. Marika and Brian told me that the workers asked if I was bringing my white nurse uniform, and white shoes?

It was an unbelievable, magical day for me.

To celebrate, Michael and Kathy arrived from Key West. And in the wonderful whiteness, there were white gifts, two matching, brand-new white couches, from Marika and Brian.

After all the celebrations were over, and the Stuart Moving Company's wonderful trucks unpacked my life, I settled down to my new surroundings and my new everyday.

Marika, Brian, and I had a "meeting" about how we will be neighbors, since they bought the condo next to mine. I asked Brian if I "embarrassed him" since I was sometimes, somewhat outspoken. He was kind and replied, "Nothing you would do would embarrass me."

There was just one thing we needed to discuss. Since my well-loved dog, Marcel, chose heaven instead of North Carolina, I had a dog problem. My kids, considering travels, and everyday life, thought it would be best if I did not get a puppy.

I thought they were right.

But I missed a dog-friend.

Three years after my breast cancer was treated successfully, and I was living happily in Winston-Salem, North Carolina, I was visiting my prior home in Indianapolis and had a call from my daughter Marika. "Your doctor at the Wake Forest Baptist Hospital has called several times. Please get in touch with him."

The hospital, just about five minutes from our homes, is a wonderful blessing, as was my doctor. His news, when I called him, was not. While replacing some missing photos from my former hospital, they found a new problem—kidney cancer.

Being so happy in my new life, this was not a good news day.

The kidney cancer doctor joined my breast cancer doctor and their STRONG suggestion was surgery, as soon as possible.

I could not believe my ears. I did NOT have to have surgery for my breast cancer, why for this? "Surgery," I announced, scared as a rabbit.

The doctors explained the alternative.

"No surgery," I answered.

As the doctors left the office, Marika and Brian were kind and explained things further. And they asked me, "Would you like to go to New York and see some plays?"

"No surgery."

"Would you like a cruise to Alaska?"

"No surgery."

"What about a trip to Hungary?"

Almost, but "No surgery."

Then Brian looked at me and asked, "Would you like a DOG?"

And I did.

On a lovely day, Marika and I were in a pet store, and even knowing that I really wanted a rescued dog, there was a puppy sitting in a cage, smiling at us, a schnoodle.

What magic led us to that place, on that day, to that dog? From the moment I saw him, I knew he was MY dog, even if he were not white to match my condo. We happily got him all his "dog things" and all the way home in the car we played "name the pup."

Nothing worked, except naturally, the name of my surgeon, Dr. Jack Smith III.

And Jack was loved by us, and by all the human neighbors at Tar Branch Towers, even if not too much by the other dogs. For over ten years, Jack was my best, adored friend. We walked through the neighborhood every day. Until he was stronger than I, and almost pulled us both, from pure curiosity, under a car on the street.

Several people from the neighborhood were interested in taking Jack, but when I told this to my son, Michael, in Key West, he said, "We will be there in two days to get Jack."

And they were…and he is the luckiest Jack.

He has his own Facebook page, to keep in touch with all of us who miss him. In a contest in Key West, he won second place for "cutest dog in Key West." He lives with loving people and four cats, walks by the shoreline, and swims in the ocean every day!

I am so happy for him.

And I, after using up seventeen boxes of Kleenex, still love and miss him.

I keep trying to tell myself that I am a grown-up now.

# 3rd christmas on the 1st floor

**HAPPY, HAPPY CHRISTMAS** from North Carolina, where the skies are Carolina blue, and the Christmas wreath on my balcony blinks happily over the red geranium, still sprouting buds.

It's difficult to believe that this is my third Christmas since Stuart's wonderful movers deposited "my life" in this condominium I now call home. And love, love, love. I love its whiteness, its openness, its high ceilings with exposed pipes, its perfect size.

I am proud that it was featured in *Winston-Salem Magazine*, and got honorable mention in my favorite magazine *Metropolitan Home's 2009 Home of the Year Issue*, and very sad that it was just prior to this wondrous magazine's demise.

I have great, adventurous neighbors, who also bravely chose urban living in downtown Winston-Salem. We are in the neighborhood of "Old Salem," with plentiful, glorious fall foliage.

The UNCSA School of the Arts, offering drama, music, and fabulous ballet is just south of us, the Symphony to the north.

The oldest women's college in the country, Salem College, is also close by, with smiling Salem sisters around us.

There is a new indie movie theater within walking distance, the A/perture, offering the new interesting films that we read about in the *New York Times*, and there is a bakery on the corner, Camino.

On every month's first Monday are my very favorite meetings of the "Dudley Shearburn Literary Society"… our book club, where I meet the most interesting and smart women. Thanks to our hostess and host, Nancy and Bucky.

We have a wonderful restaurant in our building called the Meridian, a constant reminder of a great street in Indianapolis. On Wednesdays and Fridays, we often meet neighbors at the bar there, as well as people who live in the city and are curious about Winston's new downtown.

My grown-up children are grown up…and they are wonderful. All three came (with spouses) when I moved here—it was such joy.

Marika and Brian live in the country outside Winston-Salem, but also have a condo NEXT to me…such fun.

Michele is in Indianapolis; their youngest William is as well, at Park Tudor. The rest of the Noel boys are scattered about: Jerome graduated from Hamilton, got a masters from Cornell, and works in NYC. Patrick, much to our joy, is a sophomore at Wake Forest University HERE, and Christopher is a senior in boarding school in Kent, Connecticut.

My son, Michael, and his wife, Kathy, live in Key West, Florida. This Christmas, that is where I will be, soaking up their lovely sun. And, Christmas Eve, there will be six Winston friends joining me at Michael and Kathy's yearly party in Key West.

What fun!

# my bestest friend becomes a doctor

*Marni and Dick on a visit to Winston-Salem*

**May 15, 2016, New York, NY**
A posting on Facebook:

Here I go: the city is magic, my friends are a joy....and even when there is a fire on the 46th floor of the Park Lane Hotel, and we are totally exhausted, sitting in Harry's Bar, waiting for the elevator to magically announce an opening, still I am happy, because my bestest friend of 30-some years is sitting across from me, reassuring me that the world is still wonderful.

We have been friends for 32 years, and have gone on our crazy theater trips to New York four times a year—that's 128 absolutely, unbelievable, wonderfully wondrous, JOYOUS journeys to worship in the cathedrals-called-theaters on Broadway....and off Broadway. That would be six plays a trip...right? Yes, right!

There are not too many people who would be willing to find plays on Mondays, but we always found one. Not too many people who wanted to rush in 99-degree heat, or below-freezing snow and ice, not to mention pouring rain from matinee to evening performances on Saturdays and Sundays. Some people preferred to eat. We preferred the plays.

The hours between "curtains" were pretty wonderful, too. We became very "girlie," for which in our real lives (family and work) there was not much time. But OH, the joy of looking at Bergdorf's amazingly beautiful jewelry counters, and the hunts for the wildest-color lipsticks at Bloomingdale's, Barney's and Henri Bendels made us feel very grown up and sophisticated. Getting our faces "done" and laughing until it hurt at our images in the mirrors because basically, this was really NOT us....

The museums…the MOMA, the Met, the Guggenheim, the Whitney…and our favorites as of late, The Museum of Arts and Design and the Neue Gallery, filled with adored Klimt paintings, oh my. And at the bookstores in the museums, the most alluring of all the temptations were the heavenly art books, too heavy to carry home, but not to ship home.

When there was time, or after the theater—great restaurants. Sneaking in at 21 in blue jeans, getting a tour of Per Se because we knew the designer's Hungarian name, seeing friends at Sardi's, and enjoying late night concerts at the Carlyle…

Such memories!

After all these years, we are wondering why we did not keep a journal of at least the plays. But *ah, youth*…on those bygone amazing long weekends, we forgot to think about keeping tab. We forgot the real world, our jobs, our divorces. We did let our families know we were thinking of them, and we were.

All this began when on a happy day she walked into my life.

In 1984, at the Mallons' downtown Gallery of Frame Designs, the establishment where I worked as director, part of my job was calling on established businesses to acquaint them with our wonderful being. It was difficult work, so I began with firms I knew something about. A young friend's family had a bank, and my friend's sister had the corner office. *Great*, I thought, but it was not. A lovely, young dragon lady would not even let me close to my goal.

So, I called my friend Kevin and whined....

He came through, as nice friends do.

"Marni and her husband just bought a house, and could use some art," he said and as promised he also brought his sister to the gallery to look at art...and we did. Within days I was at their new house with a load of art, along with my wisdom, which was not necessarily useful. Amazingly she did not throw me out!

Since then, we have worked on a goodly number of houses together, searching antique shops, carrying (sometimes VERY) heavy magical finds, rushing around to meet due-dates and always, always loving the challenges and saddened by the finished projects, because they were finished and we loved them, and we loved working on them.

We lived through joys and sorrows, through health and scary-named non-health problems. Her glorious curly brown hair turned gray and I was no longer the "red frog" of my childhood, with my snow-white head. We retired, I moved away to be near my daughter, but we stayed close. She came to visit in North Carolina, we still meet in New York, and we still decorate houses, but we no longer carry furniture.

We loved each other's families. She came to Florida for my son's wedding, was friends with my daughters, and heard all about my grandsons. I loved her parents, her husband, her sister and brothers, and their offspring, and her cats. And I loved HER.

She—who could do anything—was CEO of a bank, president of the family foundation, member of more boards than I can count…

She—who on May 7, 2018, received a doctorate from my alma mater, Marian University, for all the wonderful things she did and does (which I don't have room to list and she would NOT let me, anyway)…

She—the drama major who ran a bank with great success…

She—who has an artist's soul and an angel's taste…

She—who is willing to see six plays in a row rather than eat…

…is my best friend.

She and her husband still walk everywhere. They walk the wide world, seeing the most beautiful spots, always travelers, never tourists.

They walk in New York, too.

On our most recent trip to the golden city, closer to my eighty-sixth birthday than my eighty-fifth, we still saw six plays. One more glorious than the other. And, after the end of each wonderful play, there was a shiny black town car waiting to whisk me back to the hotel.

They, however, walked.

An amazing gift from my amazing friend and her amazing husband. Amazing!

And a message on my computer, waiting for me at home, "Hi, Blades, I miss you already."

I am a lucky duck.

Lolly and I were famous in the *Indianapolis Star*

## real, real friends

**ON MAY 10, 2018,** I revisited my beloved Indianapolis again.

So many happy and sad parts of my life came hurdling by me.

But the visit was full of joyous memories, and some of the most important people of my life.

One of my grandsons (representing all four of them), Christopher Kilczer, had an exhibit of his art work. It was wonderful!

His mother, Michele, was of course there.

His Uncle Michael was in town too.

I stayed at my dearest friend Lolly's lovely home.

Some sixty years of friendship with Lolly kicked off when we "did" the fabulous L.S. Ayres store windows in our youth. Well, we were called "fashion coordinators" for display. We dressed the figures for the windows, and gathered their accessories, jewelry, and whatever they needed. It was the most happy of jobs; the magical store was ours to explore.

On Mondays Ayres was closed, and we wandered in the dark store, all of our "stuff" for the windows already selected, signed out, and ready for their places in the windows. Working for the amazing, brilliant Liz Patrick (she of the PERFECT taste) and the demanding perfectionist, Mrs. Isobel Selmer (who later became a wondrous friend) was a master class. A class that required us to wear hats, and gloves, to work!

Lolly was with me when my husband, Bill, was invited to serve our country. She was there with Kleenex, and handkerchiefs for me, until I was able to join Bill in Germany. She was there with an arm full of clothes for me, when our house caught on fire, and I lost all mine to the flames.

And she is Michele's godmother.

She was there for my sixtieth birthday and painted twenty-four plates with my family's coat of arms for a wonderful gift at a wonderful party. And she was there for many perfect just party-parties. She was there for my joining the Junior League; she was there for Michele and my joining the Dramatic Club.

She was always there for me.

Thank you, Lollypop!

As we walked into the gallery for Chris's show, the first person I saw was my friend, Tony, with his beautiful daughter, Jackie. He said, "I have been waiting for an hour" and, of course, I had to start crying.

Tony was a most amazing helper of young artists and some older ones, too (like me). Since I moved away from Indianapolis, he has organized two exhibits for my paintings in Indianapolis.... not just an exhibit, but a full-blown evening with beautiful bar and food...with everything.

He (well, his company) moved my world for me to North Carolina. He left me with super fun memories—wonderful dinners in wonderful restaurants, Pacer Games in lovely private seats, the most elegant parties imaginable. Tony does *everything* with the most fabulous taste.

Usually two weeks before Christmas, he would call and say, "Time to re-decorate!" And we did…we changed art, furniture, and lamps. We had couches re-upholstered, and heaven knows what, in his house, so we were always ready for his beautiful, glorious, huge Christmas parties.

Since then, I was able to help his daughter, Jackie, decorate her fab new home, with love!

Thinking of those days, I miss Rita, his wife, my lovely friend, who retired to heaven.

Remembering all those times and magical Christmas presents, I thank you, my bestest brother, Tony!

*My friend Tony*

## return with all three

**BILL BLADES AND I** were unbelievably blessed with three unbelievable, wonderful children, who grew up into unbelievable, wonderful grown-ups.

We waited for Michele for four years, and then for sixteen hours. She was to be a boy, named after my father, Mihaly—Michael. She weighed five pounds and became Michele, the first-born beautiful daughter.

Marika was in a hurry; she arrived a year later and almost in the hospital elevator, not waiting for the doctor. She was to be named Michael also, but we happily gave her a Hungarian name, Marika. She was as lovely as her name.

Four years after Marika was born, I thought I had the flu. It turned to be—*yes*, an eight-pound red-haired BOY, whom we could finally call Michael Donner Blades after my father and Bill's mother. My dream became a reality. I had a perfect son.

And grow up they did.

Michele was in the last graduating class of Ladywood, was the cheerleading captain at Brebeuf, spent her junior year in England while at Indiana University and then went to Smith College. Marika landled leading roles in the theater at Cathedral High School and Vassar College, which she attended. Michael, following her at Cathedral and managing their football team, worked at our beloved pharmacy, Hamakers, on weekends, and in time followed the family custom of joining the Sigma Nu fraternity while at Purdue University.

Then they each got married, in as different weddings as possible:

Michele's wedding was formal, at a lovely church, with the reception at the Athletic Club, six bridesmaids, beautiful....

Marika got married on Peaks Island, Maine, in a garden, in a $49 dress, with their friend KT handling the drums, and one little flower girl... reception, beautiful....

Michael's wedding was in Key West, Florida, by the ocean, in white. Kathy wore a wonderful Italian painted gown; their beloved puppy, India, was the ring bearer...barefoot reception, beautiful....

Through their lives, they all shared special gifts with me.

Michele and Jerome:

Of course the four grandsons, H. Jerome III, Patrick, Christopher Kilczer, and William, smart and handsome (and not just in a grandmother's eyes)—what a gift! Then the Indianapolis visits. And Michele's beautiful handiwork, mostly pretty, embroidered baby and little girl dresses. For me, she crafted an amazing copy of my boarding school uniform on an American doll. And she took part in, and become the president of my favorite club, the Dramatic Club.

Brian and Marika:

Marika's amazing work at the Phoenix Theatre, and her becoming a member of Actors Equity. Then there was Brian's phone call: "I got you your Saks Fifth Avenue" when he and his brother decided to open a store in Indianapolis. Marika's kind, wonderful e-mails. Brian becoming my chief computer technician and everything else master helper. Their unbelievable generosity. More than an extra decade of life for me! A beautiful habitat that

*Michele and Jerome, Jr.*

*Marika and Brian*

*Michael and Kathy*

in the world (for me at least), the Hungarian Parliament. We were invited to a party there by my friends, Janos and Linda.

It was magical. Around thirty-five guests walked up the ninety-five red-carpeted steps. The lights were ALL lit as we walked by St. Istvan's crown of Hungary and the gilded walls surrounded us. We enjoyed a lovely group gathering, cocktails, and then a tour of the building, including even the chambers where Hungary's futures were discussed....

It was quite a beginning to the visit...wonderful memories of bygone years.

Next we visited the Hero's Square, with its magnificent sculptures of Arpád and his chieftains, who in year 895 arrived from their nomad lives to settle in this glorious spot, which they named Hungary. This place is especially meaningful to me, since my family (on my mother's side) goes back to Arpad, the Kende (king) to Kendeffy (son of Kende).

Szentes.

Dinners.

My family meeting my best friend from the second grade, *Ebe*, now white-haired, but with the same smile, with her husband, Pista, and daughter named (YES!) Márta.

Joy and laughter.

The beautiful "New York Café," where my father took me when I was in boarding school in Budapest.

The boarding school, by the city park, on *Ajtosi Durer sor*, the *Erzsébet Noiskola* (named after Elizabeth, queen of Hungary).

The Gundel Restaurant, where I remembered lovely dinners with my parents. It was reborn via

*The Hungarian Parliament*

two Americans, Ronald Lauder and George Lang in 1992.

The evening boat ride on the Danube, Buda and Pest lit up—amazing.

The museums, the city park, looking down on Pest from Buda's Fishermen's Wharf, learning Hungary's history during Nazi and Soviet time at the Torture Museum.

The gypsy music at the *Réz Kakas* (copper rooster) and the Karpathian Restaurant, eating *gulyas* soup and *dobos torta*.

With my family, in the country that once upon a time was my cradle.

How blessed, how very, very fortunate am I…
THANK YOU!
THANK YOU!
THANK YOU!

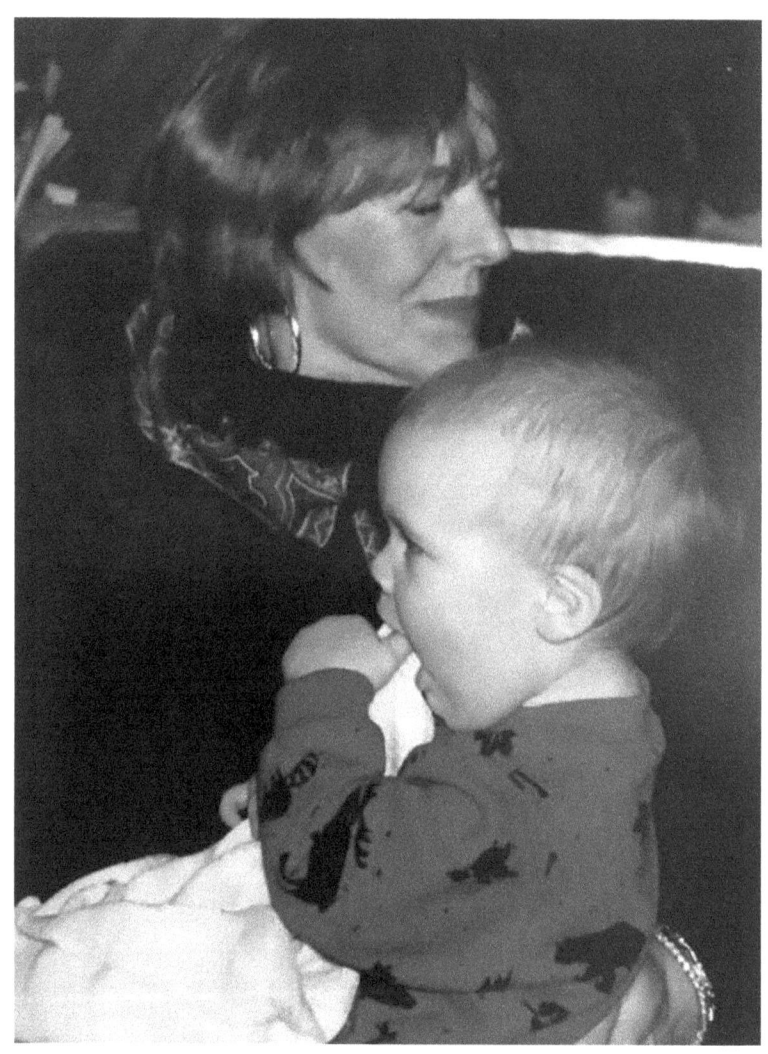

*Márta with one of her grandsons, remembering...*

## remembering

**EIGHTY-EIGHT YEARS** unfolded in such few chapters, chapters, that were not pre-planned but just happened. So many happy, and some difficult, hours passed during these eighty-eight years.

But I do not regret any.

There were some not-necessarily-important minutes…some, a kindness of strangers, some not; yet strangely they left a mark in my mind.

*Remembering:*

The Blue Note in Chicago. Bill Blades loved jazz, as did I. Nat King Cole was singing; we were in heaven. During the intermission I looked down, and the most beautiful male hand lay on the table. Yes, it was Mr. King Cole, looking at us with a glorious smile, and he asked, "Could I borrow a cigarette?" Of course he could, and a chair by our table, leaving the memory of a lovely, magical gentleman.

*Remembering:*

My childhood torturer, Laci, who called me "red frog." He was able to flee from Hungary in 1948. Our mothers were good friends, and mine told his that if Laci could ever leave, "we" (my mother) would help him as much as we could. He knew that I was in school in Lindau. By this time, I had graduated from the *Englisches Institut* and was living in Reutlingen. In Reutlingen I received a letter adressed:

Miss Márta Kilczer
Girls' School, Lindau, Germany

German post's brilliance...it was forwarded.

And Laci found us, and my mother took care of him, and he became sort of my brother. A few years later he was visiting my mother in Oil City, and he asked my mother for my hand in marriage. By then, I was enjoying receiving white roses and wearing proudly a Sigma Nu pin.

Laci finished college and worked very successfully at the Voice America for twenty-five years. We stayed in touch. The last time I saw him, he was sitting on the "family" side, with his lovely wife, at my daughter Michele's wedding.

*Remembering:*

Marika's husband, Brian, worked as U.S. Supreme Court Chief Justice Warren Burger's clerk after he graduated from Harvard Law School, so the justices were not totally unknown to him.

A few years later, Marika and Brian moved to Washington, DC, and Brian became Assistant Solicitor General. He represented the United States and its agencies in front of the Supreme Court. I was amazed. He had personally argued six cases in front of the Supreme Court, as in *the justices* whose photo appeared in the newspapers, every year, on the first Monday in October.

Marika and Brian invited me to watch his work at the Supreme Court.

I, who some years ago had arrived in the U.S. and was given $3.00 by the Red Cross...sitting in the same room with the Supreme Court!

Brian was amazing. He had the gray and black morning suit on (something worn only by lawyers from his office) and his beautiful light-blond hair was arranged in a ponytail. Ponytail?

I doubt that ponytails were seen often on lawyers in the Supreme Court. He is a very special lawyer and on that day, he looked at all those serious justices, presented his story beautifully, and he even made them laugh…and he won! There was not a more proud mother-in-law in that chamber than I.

*Remembering:*

Michele's family spent the summers at Walloon Lake in Michigan. Ernest Hemingway's family did also. His sister, Sunny, was the only one who lived there still. She adored my son-in-law, Jerome, and Michele too. When their first boy, Jerome III, was born, Sunny invited them. She wanted to see the baby. She approved. She said, "This child has a beautifully shaped head. I wonder what is in there…."

Sunny would be pleased. He is grown up now and his head is perfect, in both departments: in looks and in mind. He is a graduate of Hamilton and holds a masters from Cornell. And he is so polite. I would list him as "perfect"…of course I am his grandmother.

*Remembering:*

Marika and Brian moved to New York State. He worked in the city, and she was on the Board of Signature Theatre Company—fabulous theatre, with wonderful, serious actors and playwrights.

And when one of their playwright turned seventy, the theatre had a birthday party for him.

Edward Albee.

Marika was very involved with getting ready for this party.

And the refugee momma was invited... an unbelievable evening,

I think every "name" of the theatre-world was there. Brian and I were just looking around, watching quietly. Until Brian looked at me, and almost whispered, "Look, Arthur Miller."

It sure was. Just arriving, standing all alone. Arthur Miller!

Not for long. Brian and I welcomed him... and he was amazing! I don't need a photo of this; when I close my eyes, I can replay those minutes.

Since Marika and Brian were busy with other guests, I found an empty table and watched the "names."

Fortunately I had just seen the Frida Kahlo film, because the beautiful woman, who asked ME if she could sit down at my table was Salma Hayak, who is the heart of the film, who is as wonderful, as beautiful, as natural, and as dear in "real" life, and who spent most of the evening with me...with me....

*Remembering:*

My son, Michael, lives in Key West. He loves his town, and he is involved in many projects there. The Key West Literary Seminar is one. I think he has attended the Seminar for twenty-five years now, and he is vice president of the board. My library is full with books, signed by the elite of current American authors, all gifts from Michael and Kathy.

I went to several of the Seminars, in my "more traveling" days. They were all wonderful, but one of them was very, very special.

The poet of the book *The Apple That Astonished*

*Paris*—a favorite, favorite, favorite of mine—Billy Collins, the Poet Laureate of the United States, just happened to be there.

The real, living, and walking, and talking Billy Collins is a friend of my son's, and for one evening I thought he was mine too.

*Remembering:*

I love fashion....

And I love the fashion that my pocket cannot love.

And I love the work of a very special brilliant American designer.

Oscar de la Renta.

Of course, I do not have a De La Renta outfit.

So I had to go in a Klein suit, which I cherished.

Because I was invited...to a dinner, that Brian's generous brother, Brad, had in Memphis for Mr. Oscar de la Renta.

Heaven....

He was an amazing delight.

I had just seen *Full Gallop* in New York, a wonderful play about Diane Vreeland, who was editor of both *Harper's Bazaar* some years ago and *Vogue*, a full of ideas, brilliant, amazing woman.

Mr. de la Renta of course had known her, and had seen the play too...and he loved her, and the play too.

And among the audience during the performance that I saw was the current editor of one of the fabulous fashion magazines. I watched her. She did not laugh, or clap, or move. The taste of this editor is not mine. It was on the tip of my tongue to share my feelings with Mr. de la Renta when he smiled, and said, "She is one of my best friends."

we designed together, and the fun of their keeping a condo next to mine, to stay in often, from their country house. Countless dinners, trips, presents, for "aging pretty girls," adventures, and pure loving JOY.....

Michael and Kathy:

Lovely vacations in Key West, keeping George Walker florists busy with beautiful bouquets for me, regular phone calls keeping me up on their fascinating travels to the most interesting bands of the country, and Michael's fascinating job as logistic director of RPM Nautical Foundation (finding ancient ships, and artifacts all over the world)... AND without my asking, offering a generous, wonderful retirement and a happy life for my beloved dog, Jack.

Thank you!

During my 2017 third bout of cancer, Marika and Brian were at my hospital bed every morning at 6:00 a.m. for the doctor's visit. Michele arrived from Indianapolis, and Michael from Key West, finding their mother NOT being her charming best....

Thank you!

They all gathered for my eightieth birthday at beautiful Blackberry farm in Tennessee, a weekend I will never forget...pure joy!

Thank you!

And, and, and—making my forever dream come true... a trip with all three of my grown children (and spouses) to my beautiful birth-country, HUNGARY.

Oh! Thank you!

We arrived at the Budapest airport around 3:00 p.m. and asked the taxi-driver to please hurry us to the Sofitel hotel, because at 6:00 p.m. we were to be at a side entrance of the most beautiful building

I will be forever grateful for that smile, AND for his speaking faster than I. I almost learned to think before I speak. Almost.

*Remembering:*

While Marika and Brian lived in New York, Michael and Kathy, and Michele and her boys, and I spent wonderful time with them there.

On one weekend when we were all together in the city, Brian had one request: "Please let's NOT see *Annie Get Your Gun* and *Minelli on Minelli*, Liza Minelli's solo concert. Not knowing this, Michele already had tickets for *Annie*, and we went to see it. Brian was kind and understanding.

In New York, my favorite restaurant is Joe Allen, in the theater district. It is not a fancy restaurant, but it is usually filled with theater people after curtain. I love to see them, and sometimes catch a few words from their tables. And I try to be polite, not to stare, and of all things not to run after them, or bother them. So much I can do and not shame my family.

But this time, I could not have possibly just sat there behaving like a lady. She was walking toward us, with her entourage.

I was up, and could not believe my eyes…
Liza Minelli.
And she hugged me…
Marika said, "*We* are going to see Liza tomorrow."
And we did.
And it was über-fabulously-wonderful.
We laughed, and cried, and decided that this was the most wonderful evening in a theater.
Brian did too. One of two is not bad….

*And these days...*

Baptized by my friend Katie, "The Wonderful Women's Wednesday Wine Club" is a happening every Wednesdays at the Meridian Restaurant in Winston-Salem. The membership changes from one Wednesday to the next, but chances are one would find Winston's grand dame, Ms Phyllis, there. She is the beloved retired English teacher whose students, now grown up, and some quite famous, stop by just to see *her*, along with many lovely neighbors and visitors from all over. We are grateful that she keeps us up on the amazing schedule of the happenings at the UNCSA (University of North Carolina School of the Arts)—be it Theater, Dance, or Music, it is always superb. Knowing more about Winston-Salem than most, she shares its stories with joy.

*The Wonderful Women's Wednesday Wine Club*

And: Next to the women's club, we often find favorite neighbors Adolfo, Kevin, Tom, Milton and Corby, my new best friend, the artist Avy, who is five years old, Ms. Alli at the bar, and Chef Mark, the chef-owner, at the magical kitchen The Meridian is a delight for born Winstonians and newcomers alike, including this newcomer, me.

* * *

Thank you for letting me share a few of my cherished minutes, silly or not.
I loved them.

# acknowledgments

**I WOULD NEED** a few hundred more pages to list my gratitudes. Here are just a few. First of all, I turn toward heaven, thankful for everything.

Yes, it does take a village, or a few cities, those wonderful worlds and people in them. In Indianapolis, Indiana, there's Marian College (now University); Editions Limited Gallery; and an old house on Park Avenue. In Winston-Salem, North Carolina, we have Wake Forest Baptist Medical Center; Tar Branch Towers; Exhibits at Meridian; Willows; Sawtooth Art School; and Salem College. And in Asheville, the Old Europe Bakery, where the Hungarian pastries inspired us as we gave birth to "ze book."

And: I thank my grown children and their spouses, who in many thoughtful ways and words, made these pages possible: Michele and Jerome Jr., Marika and Brian, Kathy and Michael, you are amazing, kind, and generous. I will never be able to thank you enough and to love you enough.

And: Marni and Dick, for their never-ending friendship, for their reading this manuscript on a very busy trip to New York, and for reassuring me with their enthusiasm.

And: Citrine Publishing, my publisher Penelope Love, is brilliant, brilliant, a magician. She understood my silly wishes that even I could not understand. Working with her was pure joy! (As was her family, Nick and Liebchen.) She has my forever thanks.

And: My special gratitude, a *köszönöm* ("thank you" in Hungarian) goes to my extraordinary, super-smart friend, Gail Fisher, for her time, her encouragement, her patience, her kindness, for making the best gazpacho, knowing where to put the commas, and making it all such fun.

Thank you, Y'ALL!

*My happy future, Sisi*

## possibility of a future

**AND NOW THE TIME** has come to close the door to the past...

...and open the sunshiny, glorious, hopeful door to the future.

*The Future* is an adorable kitten friend who just walked into my life: Sisi, named after the beautiful Empress Elizabeth of Austria and Queen of Hungary. She changed my world from every-day to Sis-land.

And...

Four adorable little boys, who each stole my heart forever: my grandsons.

Michele and Jerome Jr.'s amazing sons:

Jerome III, Patrick, Christopher Kilczer, and William.

They are all grown up now, graduated from colleges, out in the real world, making it better.

They are young Americans, of whom I am very proud.

This book is for THEM...

A reminder that once upon a time, they had a grandmother, who loved two countries: these glorious, wonderful United States of America and a beautiful, small country, across the ocean, fighting over a thousand years for its life: Hungary.

And they had an Hungarian-born grandmother who loves them.

*With me and my dog, Marcel, before they grew up*

*Patrick, Jerome III, Christopher Kilczer, and William*

"There is a future which—tomorrow, later, next century—will be. There is a future which is predictable, programmed, scheduled, foreseeable. And there is a future, *l'avenir* (to come) which refers to someone who comes whose arrival is totally unexpected. For me, that is the real future… the totally unpredictable."

—jacques derrida

www.ingramcontent.com/pod-product-compliance
Lightning Source LLC
Chambersburg PA
CBHW041302240426
43661CB00010B/998